Astrology For You

Astrology is not a complex scier
and, in the hands of the world-famous 'human computer
Shakuntala Devi, it becomes yet simpler and easier to
understand and practise. The present book discusses
zodiacs, pla ets, asterisms, the rising signs, Bhavas,
Yogas, Dasas and their effects and transits. It enables
the reader to cast a horoscope, and also read one. There
are tables of correction for various cities and for
sidereal time, Nakshatra divisions and Vimshottari
Dasa, Navamsas, etc. It is a complete book that leaves
nothing to become an amateur astrologer.

Shakuntala Devi, though well-known as a
mathematical genius the world over, is essentially an
astrologer, now practising in Bombay and Delhi. She
learnt this science in the lap of her grandfather when
quite young; hers is a well-known family of priests and
astrologers in South India. This is her first important
book on the subject aimed at the layreader and
presented in a style that is easy to follow.

By the same author
in
Orient Paperbacks

ASTROLOGY
FOR YOU

Shakuntala Devi

Orient
Paperbacks
DELHI | MUMBAI | HYDERABAD

www.orientpaperbacks.com

ISBN 13: 978-81-222-0067-6
ISBN 10: 81-222-0067-2

1st Published 1983
17th Printing 2011

Astrology For You

Cover design by C.V. Gurunathan
for Vision Studio

Published by
Orient Paperbacks
(A division of Vision Books Pvt. Ltd.)
5A/8, Ansari Road, New Delhi-110 002

Printed in India at
Saurabh Printers Pvt. Ltd., Noida

Cover Printed at
Ravindra Printing Press, Delhi-110 006

"It is fortune, not wisdom, that rules man's life."

— CICERO

"Like the winds of the seas are the ways of fate,
As we voyage along through life,
'Tis the set of the soul
That decides its goal,
And not the calm or the strife"

— DRYDEN

"One ship drives east and another drives west
With the self sale winds that blow;
'Tis the set of the sails
And not the gales
Which tell us the way to go."

— ELLA WHEELER WILCOX

Foreword

In this book I have provided various guidelines to bring Astrology within the easy grasp of the layman. I have explained in this book the main principles of drawing up the birth charts according to the Indian System as well as the Western System, to appraise the birth charts as well as to judge timings of events on the basis of planetary periods and sub-periods, and transits.

I have tried to present, in this book, authentic Astrological information, and its practical application to the needs of humanity.

While I have given an outline of the fundamental concepts of Astrology according to Indian System as well as the Western System, I have also explained the workings of both the systems. For the sake of sheer efficiency, I have explained the mathematical portion of Astrology according to Western System, and then, if need be, the result converted to Indian System.

Theoretical knowledge of Astrology only is not sufficient for one to master the subject. It is through practise, and practise alone, that one can gain more and more practical knowledge of Astrology. Experience, after all, is the best instructor.

Shakuntala Devi

Contents

What is Astrology?

Astrology is the science that describes the influence of the heavenly bodies upon mundane affairs and upon human character and life. The oldest science in existence, it is the science of the effects of the Solar Currents on the living things of our earth, especially on human life.

Knowledge is power! And Astrology is the master key to the lock of truth. By knowing what our destiny indicates and by knowing what pitfalls lie ahead of us, and the courses which threaten disaster, we can exercise our choice to determine the best course to avert the catastrophe. To be forewarned is to be forearmed!

The horoscope indicates the pattern on which life is built. The stars indicate what will come to pass. But with intelligence and free will one can change the natural course of events.

The wise man cooperates with the stars and by doing so adds to his own happiness, efficiency and usefulness in the world.

But the fool thinks that he rules the stars!

Astrology points out the potentialities, capabilities and limitations of the individual. But how far we shall

9

develop the desirable traits and overcome those which are undesirable, depends upon the exercise of "Free will". Astrology shows the way and it is for us to decide whether we have to follow the path and maintain a balance between the mental and the physical.

Astrology points out the weak spots in our character and shows us the reason why we are not successful in our endeavours in life. When we are in danger of suffering due to our weaknesses and when misfortune is likely to overtake us, Astrology gives us a forewarning.

Through Astrology it is possible for us to ascertain for what kind of work we are best fitted, and the times and seasons when opportunity will be presented for establishing ourselves in that work.

When we attempt to arrive at a solution for our problems, it is essential to study man in his relation to the universe. Embedded in the structure of the cosmos is the law of fatality. Life is a chain of successive causes and effects link upon link. But whereas fatality is the process of nature, freedom is the essence of human nature. And free will is the highest possession of a human being.

Free will makes a man a moral being. In fact morality is always a choice among alternatives. Otherwise there would be fatalism, helplessness, irresponsibility, leaving no justification for the punishment of crime or for paying the penalty of ignorance or wrong doing, and on the other hand, for awarding merit to intelligence and virtue.

In his essay on human nature, Charles Fleischer quotes "Animal nature plus vision, plus will, equals human nature".

Some of us who are ready to accept fatality as finality only use it as a defence mechanism—an inclination to blame the stars and circumstances as the ultimate determining forces and factors of our lives.

Fatalism only exists on the material plane. The soul is not shackled by fate. Astrology can only indicate what is likely to happen, but no astrologer is qualified to determine how the events which are preordained shall influence each individual. This depends on the individual's own free will and the degree of development he has attained and which will determine his mental attitude towards anything which may happen. One can hope to receive results through one's opportunities in proportion to the use one makes of them.

Astrology points out the best and shortest and safest route to a given goal. It offers solutions to our problems. It reveals us to ourselves—our physical and psychical make up, our tendencies and our possibilities.

Astrology makes it possible for us to analyze and diagnose ourselves. And with the help of Astrology, we may use our intelligence and free will both to avert dangers and to convert opportunity to our advantage. It throws open wide fields of valuable knowledge, and enlarges our sphere of consciousness. It enables us to be master, rather than servant, dictator, rather than victim of circumstances.

Fate knocks at the door. But it is upto us to bid her enter or keep her out.

The fatalists are those who drift with the tide or oppose it, instead of adjusting their course to the ebb and flow by exercising intelligent free will.

Astrology is the emancipator from ignorance which helps the individual to understand himself, and also to understand one's fellowmen better, and to be more

11

sympathetic and more tolerant.

Life is evolution fostered by vision and will. The balance between fatalism and free will is suggested by self direction and self-control. Man, the individual is the free arbiter of his fate through the use of vision, intelligence and will.

The Zodiac

Sun and the moon move among the stars along a belt, and they do not go beyond a certain width on either side of the central line of motion. All the planets confine their lateral movements to this belt. This belt is known as the Zodiac.

The Zodiac is circular in shape, and the circumference of the Zodiacal belt contains 360 degrees; consequently each house or sign contains thirty degrees. The twelve equal parts, called signs of the Zodiac, are represented, by imaginary figures, and they affect the body, the character, the disposition and the mental and moral attributes, as well as possibilities for success or failure of a human being. The twelve signs, which are also called houses, describe the environment and circumstances, the possibilities and limitations of every phase of destiny with which each individual is confronted in his voyage through life !

The houses of the Zodiac are represented by the chart in a horoscope. In order to determine the importance and strength of any particular house, it is necessary to examine, first, the lord of that house and his aspects. Secondly, any planets that may be present in that house, and their aspects. Thirdly, and of the greatest importance, is to examine whether the nature of the sign is itself sympathetic to that of the house.

In the Hindu system of Astrology, the chart is in the form of a square or oblong whereas in the Western system the chart is drawn in the form of a circle.

The names of the twelve signs in the Hindu system, as well as the western system, and their symbols are as follows :

MESHA	♈	ARIES
VRISHABHA	♉	TAURUS
MITHUNA	♊	GEMINI
KARKATA	♋	CANCER
SIMHA	♌	LEO
KANYA	♍	VIRGO
TULA	♎	LIBRA
VRISCHIKA	♏	SCORPIO
DHANU	♐	SAGITTARIUS
MAKARA	♑	CAPRICORN
KUMBHA	♒	AQUARIUS
MEENA	♓	PISCES

The Zodiac is represented as follows in the Hindu system:

12. Meena	1. Mesha	2. Vrishabha	3. Mithuna
11 Kumbha			4. Karkata
10. Makara			5. Simha
9. Dhanu	8. Vrischika	7. Tula	6. Kanya

In northern and western India the chart pattern is as follows:

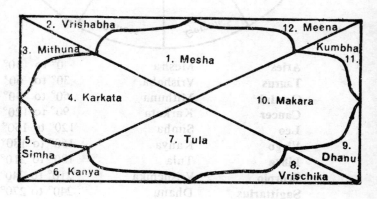

In the Western system the chart is as follows:

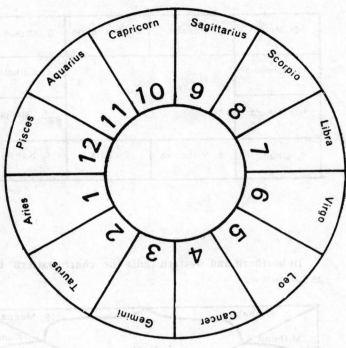

Aries	Mesha	0° to 30°
Taurus	Vrishaba	30° to 60°
Gemini	Mithuna	60° to 90°
Cancer	Karkata	90° to 120°
Leo	Simha	120° to 150°
Virgo	Kanya	150° to 180°
Libra	Tula	180° to 210°
Scorpio	Vrishchika	210° to 240°
Sagittarius	Dhanu	240° to 270°
Capricorn	Makara	270° to 300°
Aquarius	Kumbha	300° to 330°
Pisces	Meena	330° to 360°

The Twelve Houses

When a person is born, or an incident occurs, a certain point or degree of one of the twelve signs of the Zodiac will be rising on the Eastern horizon. This rising sign is called the Ascendant, and in the Hindu system it is known as the Lagna.

The character of a person and also the course of his life will largely depend upon this rising sign. In order to determine the first house, or the rising sign, the exact hour of birth is very necessary. The lack of accuracy of the time of birth, may result in errors of judgement in diagnosing a horoscope.

Even a slight abscence of harmony r ay interfere with the perfect operation of a powerful configuration.

The horoscope is a chart indicating the positions of the sun, the moon and seven planets in relation to the earth and to the Zodiac for any given moment of time.

The twelve houses of the horoscope that govern a man's life, in its different aspects are as follows:

Ascendant

The first house, which mundanely is Aries or Mesha is ruled by Mars. It signifies man's outward appearance like personality, body, environment at birth and other physical aspects. It rules head and the face and determines the degree of activity or repression of the individual.

House of Wealth

The second house, which mundanely is Taurus is ruled over by Venus. It signifies a man's financial circumstances, profit or gain, loss or damage and all his movable goods. It rules the neck and the throat and determines the degree of prosperity, which the individual will enjoy in life.

The House of Relatives

The third house which mundanely is Gemini is ruled over by Mercury. It signifies brothers, sisters, neighbours, environment of the family, short journeys, correspondence and messages, the degree of mentality, perception and adaptability of the individual, and determines his relations with all these departments. It rules the shoulders, arms, hands and fingers.

The House of the Home

The fourth house, which mundanely is Cancer, is ruled over by the moon. It signifies the father or mother, inherited tendencies, the environment during the early childhood and old age, and landed property. It rules the stomach and breast and determines the native's relations with his father and mother, environment, and the state of his property holdings.

The House of Pleasure

The fifth house, which mundanely is Leo, is ruled over by the Sun. It signifies love affairs, entertainment, speculation and children of the individual. It rules the heart and back, and determines the degree of success or failure of the native's love affairs and pleasures, his speculative operations, and matters concerning his offspring.

The House of Health

The sixth house, which mundanely is Virgo is ruled over by Mercury. It signifies the needs, afflictions, and care of the body, servants, inferiors, dress and hygiene, grand parents, uncles and aunts and domestic animals of the individual. It rules the intestines and solar plexus and determines the state of the native's health, his ability to get on with servants and inferiors, and his relations with grand parents, uncles and aunts and small animals.

The House of Marriage

The seventh house which mundanely is Libra is ruled over by Venus. It signifies marriage, business—partnerships and enemies of the individual. It rules the veins, the kidneys, in the case of a woman the ovaries and determines the degree of happiness and success the native derives through marriage and partnership, and the type of enemies the native may have.

The House of Death

The eighth house which mundanely is Scorpio, is ruled over by Mars. It signifies the inheritance, legacies, wills and the goods of deed of the individual. It rules the organs of generation and determines all questions regarding inheritance, and the type of death of the native.

The House of Religion and Philosophy

The ninth house, which mundanely is Sagittarius, is ruled over by Jupiter. It signifies religion, philosophy, long journeys, particularly by water, and the relations with foreigners of the individual. It rules over abstract thought, dreams and visions. It also rules over the hips and thighs, determines the philosophical and religious beliefs of the native, and the amount of travel and success he will enjoy in far off countries.

The House of Business and Honour

The tenth house which mundanely is Capricorn is ruled over by Saturn. It signifies ambition, fame, worldly position, power, promotion, elevation, the calling of authority, of the individual. It rules the skeleton and knees in particular and determines the degree of success in business and the honour of the native.

The House of Friends

The eleventh house, which mundanely is Aquarius is ruled over by Uranus. It signifies the friendships and the aspirations of the individual. It rules the legs, ankles in particular, and determines the native's relation with friends, his position towards humanity, and the degree of harmony or disharmony in his relationship with his fellowmen.

The House of Secret Enemies

The twelfth house, which mundanely is Pisces is ruled over by Neptune. It signifies, unseen difficulties, impairment of the senses, seclusion, forced or otherwise and secret enemies of the individual. It rules the extremities and determines the amount of freedom enjoyed by the native. It also determines the degree to which he will be forced to submerge his own personality, in his subservience to others.

The twelve signs can be grouped as follows:

Masculine Signs : ARIES, GEMINI, LEO, LIBRA SAGITTARIUS AND AQUARIUS.

Feminine Signs : TAURUS, CANCER, VIRGO, SCORPIO, CAPRICORN, PISCES.

Fiery Signs : ARIES, LEO, SAGITTARIUS

Earthy Signs : TAURUS, VIRGO, CAPRICORN

Airy Signs : GEMINI, LIBRA, AQUARIUS

Watery Signs : CANCER, SCORPIO, PISCES

Opposites

ARIES	Opposite	LIBRA
TAURUS	Opposite	SCORPIO
GEMINI	Opposite	SAGITTARIUS
CANCER	Opposite	CAPRICORN
LEO	Opposite	AQUARIUS
VIRGO	Opposite	PISCES

The twelve signs can also be grouped as follows:

The first, fourth, seventh and the tenth houses denote the childhood of a person.

The second, fifth, eighth and the eleventh houses denote the adulthood of a person.

The third, sixth, ninth and the twelfth houses denote the old age of a person.

Houses from the first to the eighth relates to an individual's material life; Ninth to eleventh religious or moral life and the twelfth to the other world.

Following this grouping one can predict an individual's material, moral and the other life.

Planets

The names of the planets in the Hindu system, as well as the western system and their symbols are as follows:

RAVI	☉	SUN
CHANDRA	☽	MOON
KUJA	♂	MARS
BUDHA	☿	MERCURY
GURU	♃	JUPITER
SHUKRA	♀	VENUS
SANI	♄	SATURN
INDRA	♅	URANUS
VARUNA	♆	NEPTUNE

The planets rule over their assigned signs and consequently while they have great power in their own signs, they are weak in others. The assigned signs of the various planets are as follows:

	Sign		Ruling Planet
♈	ARIES	♂	MARS
♉	TAURUS	♀	VENUS
♊	GEMINI	☿	MERCURY
♋	CANCER	☽	MOON
♌	LEO	☉	SUN
♍	VIRGO	☿	MERCURY
♎	LIBRA	♀	VENUS
♏	SCORPIO	♂	MARS
♐	SAGITTARIUS	♃	JUPITER
♑	CAPRICORN	♄	SATURN
♒	AQUARIUS	♅	URANUS
♓	PISCES	♆	NEPTUNE

Their exalted, strong and weak positions may be grouped as follows:

Sign	Exalted	Strong	Weak
Aries	Sun	Mars	Saturn
Taurus	Moon	—	Sun
Gemini	—	—	—
Cancer	Jupiter	Moon	Mars
Leo	—	Sun	—
Virgo	Mercury	—	Venus
Libra	Saturn	Venus	Sun
Scorpio	—	—	Moon

Sagittarius	—	Jupiter	—
Capricorn	Mars	—	Jupiter
Aquarius	—	Saturn	—
Pisces	Venus	—	Mercury

In the exalted positions, the planets are very powerful, and with experience one can specify the exact degree where the planets attain their fullest power. Here are some examples:

Sun	in Aries	19°
Moon	in Taurus	3°
Mars	in Capricorn	28°
Mercury	in Virgo	15°
Jupiter	in Cancer	5°
Venus	in Pisces	27°
Saturn	in Libra	20°

The opposite points in the signs of the Zodiac are the degrees where the planets are extremely weak.

Amongst the planets, there are compatible planets and incompatible planets. They can be termed as friends and enemies. They are grouped as follows:

Planets	Friends	Enemies
Sun	Moon, Venus, Jupiter Neptune, Mercury	Mars, Saturn
Moon	Sun, Mercury, Venus, Jupiter, Neptune	Mars, Saturn, Uranus
Mars	Sun, Saturn	Mercury, Venus, Jupiter, Moon, Neptune, Uranus

Planets	Friends	Enemies
Mercury	Moon, Venus, Jupiter, Sun, Uranus	Mars, Saturn
Jupiter	Sun, Moon, Mercury, Venus, Neptune, Uranus	Mars, Saturn
Venus	Moon, Mercury, Jupiter, Neptune, Sun, Uranus	Mars, Saturn
Saturn	Neptune	Sun, Moon, Mercury, Venus, Jupiter, Uranus

The strength of the planets is in the following ascending order:

Uranus, Neptune, Saturn, Mars, Mercury, Jupiter, Venus, Moon and Sun.

The planets are strong while they occupy the houses of exaltation, own houses or houses of friends.

Particularly speaking Mercury and Jupiter are stronger in the first house, the Moon and Venus are strong in the fourth house, Saturn in the seventh house and the Sun and Mars in the tenth house.

Planets are weak, when they occupy the enemy houses.

Characteristics of the Planets

The Sun

The Sun is the parent body of the Solar System. The Sun rules over the sign Leo and his exaltation is in 19 degrees of Aries. He has no latitude, being always in the ecliptic and is never in the inferior state. He co-operates sympathetically with all the planets except Saturn. He is temperately hot, dry and masculine. He can be good or evil depending upon the planets in configuration with him.

The Sun is the centre and giver of all life. And as such he is the backbone of the whole system of Astrology. The moon is the giver of form and consequently the conjunction or opposition between the Sun and the Moon is malignant in the physical plane, or the same when in parallel of declination. The relationship of the Sun and Moon largely determines whether life can be expressed harmoniously or the reverse. If the aspects are friendly, our individuality and personality cooperate. And we are not confronted with the many oppositions and conflicting conditions

27

present when the Sun and Moon are unfriendly or in parallel to each other.

When the Sun is strongly placed in an individual's horoscope, particularly in his own sign Leo, in rising, the native has a large, long strong body, peircing eyes and well built person. He has broad, high forehead and light curly hair.

If the Sun is in his dignified aspect, the native is of noble disposition, proud, magnanimous and generous. He is humane, affable and a faithful friend, and a generous enemy. He is also prone to be over fond of magnificence. If the Sun is in his ill dignified aspect of the individual's horoscope, the native is foolishly proud or vain, arrogant, troublesome, stubborn, superficial, restless and uncharitable.

Where the Sun is in a dominant position of influence in the life, the will is strong and the person possesses a masterful character. And the confidence given by self-respect and cheerful outlook toward life will cause the native to attract much good fortune.

However, the native may find it necessary to guard against being too frank and outspoken, and it may be advisable for him to cultivate caution and secretiveness. He must also check his fondness for display which may, if unchecked, turn into "Exhibition Complex".

The native of this planet possesses unusual skill to look into mysteries of life to make a study of nature's finer forces, and he is also endowed with the power to rise above the station to which he is born. Others will turn to him for counsel and assistance.

Many men holding top government positions or those of high executive positons are born strongly under the influence of this planet. However, it all depends on one's sphere as to the degree and type of success attained.

The native of this planet is easily led, but he can be very stubborn and difficult to manage if he feels that he is being imposed upon.

The Sun, represents the constitution, the life principle and the character of the native. Where the influence of the Sun is strong, it enables the native to reap the rewards of favourable planetary aspects. And conversely the individual has to suffer and endure the buffets of adverse influences.

Where the Sun is weak, no amount of benefits from the other planets will counter act that affliction.

The Sun governs the back, the heart, the arteries, the eyes and the retentive faculty. His illnesses are fainting, palpitation of the heart and weak sight.

The Sun rules organic troubles and the Moon functional disorders.

The Moon

The Moon expresses personality and has rule over the sign of Cancer. It is a feminine planet which is cold, moist, watery, phlegmatic and nocturnal.

The native who has a strong influence of the moon has a fair stature, pale complexion, round face, bright eyes, short arms, thick hands and feet, smooth, corpulent and phlegmatic body. If approaching to a conjunction of the Sun, the native is likely to be of a very delicate constitution during the first four years of his life.

The moon is easily influenced by every other force and this planet is more sensitive to the influence of the signs of the Zodiac than any of the other planets. In fact what accounts for the greatest difference in two lives born only a few moments apart is the slight change in the degree on the ascendant and the position of the moon. This is the reason why twins are often so unlike each other.

Apart from the fact that the signs themselves affect the moon tremendously, the subdivisions into decades also have an equally great effect.

If the moon is in a good aspect of the individual's horoscope, the native will be mild, soft, kind, ingenuous and polite. But he will also be timid, thoughtless, unsettled. He would be totally averse to disputes or troubles of any kind.

When the moon is in an ill dignified aspect the native is bound to be idle, stupid, petty and fond of alcohol.

The moon governs the brain, the stomach, the bowels, the bladder and the left eye It also has much influence over the fluids of the body, the salion, lymphs, glands, and in case of women the breasts.

If the moon is the star of destiny of an individual, it has a strangely double quality on the influence it can have on the person. Its vibrations can produce either extreme purity and devotion to the higher things or it can make one a slave to the emotions.

People born under the strong influence of moon should choose well their associates and adopt a line of life in which discipline is rigid. Otherwise they are in danger of being lax and casual about life.

The native of this planet is extremely sensitive and naturally absorbs, all kinds of influences. Therefore the native must try to discriminate between the true and false, between things worthwhile, and those which are useless. The natives of this sign usually know of no middle paths.

The native of this planet is usually extremely adaptible and this can give him charm. He is usually versatile and he has a tendency to take advantage of opportunities. However, it can also have the opposite effect and make the native to be simply a straw to indicate which way the wind blows.

If the native exercises sufficient will power, the forces can be stabilised to overcome the tendency to diffuse one's forces.

When the moon is the dominant force, the native is prone to change the vocation chosen early in life, although it might have been the stepping stone that might have led to his true work later on. It brings in his life many changes of position and fluctuations of reputation. However, the native is not destined to lead an obscure or uneventful life. And therefore the native must so govern his affairs that any publicity which comes may be conducive to success and happiness.

This planet often brings the native, opportunities to play important parts in public affairs, politics or clubs. The moon rules the populace and as such many who enjoy great popularity and who influence the masses are born strongly under this planet. Many distinguished men involved in public affairs, are under the strong influence of this planet.

The moon also governs the home. Therefore women who are natives of this planet make excellent wives and mothers. However, they are prone to love novelty, change and sensation, and as such they often find it necessary to have a large circle of acquaintances and to be given greater freedom. Without this freedom, they are inclined to become restless and discontended with their domestic life.

The masculine natives of this planet are likely to attract wives of masculine types. There is a tendency for them to develop into being "henpecked husbands" unless they cultivate will and grow more self-assertive.

31

The moon enjoys great importance, although she is of negative influence, because she represents the sensorium. Whatever goes to man, the qualities he may possess, his ego, all these things can only come into manifestation through the medium of the senses.

An afflicted moon, regardless of other aspects in the horoscope, cuts one off from the ability to make use of all that might be promised by the other planets, and inhibits their qualities. The afflicted moon can produce afflicted sensorium sufficiently to prevent any qualities of other beneficient planets to have effect.

Being of swifter motion than the other planets the influence of the moon is of very great importance and she forms more aspects. She indicates minor incidents, circumstances, changes and all actions of daily life. She is therefore responsible for the mundane happenings which are of interest to the average men and woman.

Her diseases are consumption, rheumatism, vertigo, colic, palsy, apoplexy, seropila, small pox, dropsy and most important of all, lunacy, in its various forms.

Moon, in her bad aspect, is the most undisputed threat to the health, and can be the cause of most of the functional disorders.

Mercury

Mercury is the chief ruler of the nerve forces and mental faculties of mankind. He is always close to the Sun, never farther than twentyeight degrees, and performs his orbit in, eighty-seven days, twentythree hours.

He takes on the quality of the planets with which he is configurated, and as such he is good, or bad, lucky or unlucky.

Mercury takes on the vibration of whatever sign or planet it is aspected by.

Mercury is the ruler of Gemini and Virgo.

The person born under the strong influence of mercury is tall, straight figured, has a deep forehead, straight nose, thin lips, narrow chin, thin, narrow face, long arms, hands, fingers, thighs, legs and feet.

In its dignified aspect Mercury gives its native a strong mind, active and subtle, a retentive memory, and an eagerness in the pursuit of all kinds of knowledge. The native is a good orator, eloquent, witty and of a pleasing disposition. If however, the native has the Mercury in conjunction with Sun, then the native is more qualified for trade than for learning.

In its ill dignified aspect, when the Mercury is badly afflicted, the native will possess a mean, shuffling, unprincipled character. The native is prone to be a liar, thief, tale bearer, and gambler. He is bound to be void of any kind of useful knowledge or ability, but yet he is prone to be very conceited.

When Mercury is void of aspect with Saturn, it is very essential that the native of this planet be concrete in thought, and to avoid making promises without carefully considering the extent of commitment. It is also essential that the native should try to visualize as perfectly as possible any new project or personal interview before attempting it. If not, the native may have to cope with embarrassment and expense.

The natives of this planet find it difficult to realize that others are not as frank and as sincere as themselves. And they are therefore in danger of mistakes by being too trusting and optimistic. It is therefore imperative that the natives of this planet should not be too credulous, and even to examine all the details about those with whom they have business dealings until the latter have proved themselves worthy of their confidence.

The type of mind a native of Mercury possesses will meet with more success where inspiration, brilliancy of thought or quick action are needed, rather than concentration, method or persistency.

Mercury governs the thought centres of memory. It also governs speech, the nostrils, the hand, feet, lungs and nerves.

The diseases of the planet are usually convulsions, stammering, apoplexy, lisping, dumbness, stoppage of humour in the nose or head, nervous cough, hoarseness, gout in the hands and feet and vertigo. An afflicted Mercury can cause mental diseases.

An individual who has Mercury in an exalted position at birth, is led to choose, and he becomes distinguished in the intellectual and literary pursuits. But the native, who is unfortunate enough to have the planet afflicted at birth is likely to develop a mean and an unprincipled character. He is bound to be full of deceit, low and cunning. Amongst those who have an afflicted Mercury are many promoters of lies, swindlers, forgers and thieves.

The most truly sensitive of all the planets is Mercury. Mercury responds to every impression. And Mercury is not modified by the signs as are the more passive planets. On the other hand each sign excites him to give a special impression of opinion.

Mercury is the mind. While the contents of mind are determined by the food of the mind, yet different minds deal quite differently with identical foods.

The best influence upon Mercury is Saturn. Without the steadying hand of Saturn, to hold him in tutorship to a profounder wisdom, Mercury may be frivolous and vain. But when Mercury is overpowered by Venus, the mental qualities become subservient and slavish. And then the native of this planet does not have a mind of his own.

However, whatever aspects may exist, it will not alter the essential character of the planet.

The natives of this planet have a great desire for knowledge, the longing for change and cosmopolitan spirit. They are bound to travel far and wide. They have keen intuition and ability to sense what people are about to say. A common trait of the natives of this sign is to interrupt conversations and to change the subject so quickly that others would find it difficult to follow them. A lot will depend upon the environment and mental development of the native, whether his inquisitive nature will cause him to be curious over petty things or those of more importance. The restiveness and the tendency to be easily bored, of the native, is, often caused by his own mercurial nature, and not through the fault of people or circumstances.

Lack of ability to take decision, and a wandering mind are two of the outstanding characteristics of the native of this sign, which may prevent his permanent success.

The mind of the natives of this planet is never at rest, and because of this reason they require more rest and more sleep, than does the average person.

The natives of this planet must guard against being too introspective and should associate as much as possible with spiritually minded people.

Venus

Venus is never above fortyeight degrees distant from the Sun, and performs her orbit in two hundred and twentyfour days and seven hours. She is a tem-

35

perate planet, considered as the "Lesser fortune".

Venus is the star of destiny of those born under Taurus and Libra.

Those who have Venus in the exalted position at birth are usually elegantly formed and extremely beautiful, with sparkling eyes and round, smooth face with dimples in the cheek or chin. They usually have a wandering eye, denoting desire, sweet voice and very engaging address.

However, the amount of influence this planet will contribute towards bestowing all the above qualities on the native, largely depends on its position with regard to sign, house and aspect. For example, if Venus is friendly to the degree in the Ascendant or to Jupiter, the native will be endowed with beauty, and on the other hand if it is unfriendly to the ascendant or to any of the other planets, not only the natives appearance will be marred but also the harmony of his character will be affected.

Venus, has the effect on her native to make him pleasure loving rather superficial, and inclined to go along the line of least resistance. The native will be unwilling to make sacrifices and do the hard plodding that is essential to great accomplishment.

A badly afflicted Venus can have the effect on the native to be profligate, indolent, shameless, wholly abandoned, and open to every species of lust and depravity. However, as a rule the natives of this sign are mild and in-offensive.

When Venus is the dominating planet in the horoscope, a great deal of good fortune, in the way of favours, kindness and patronage are bestowed on the native. He will have powerful friends, who will stand by him and assist him in making his life path easy and pleasant. The native may count among his friends,

36

people in high positions or even those holding titles. Gifts and favours will be showerd upon him, just for the asking. His entire personality will attract kindness and consideration from others.

Love will play a very prominent role in the destiny of the natives of Venus, and will be a source of much happiness to them directly or indirectly.

Persons born strongly under the influence of Venus are inclined to contract early marriages, as a rule before twentyeight or thirty. However, the strong motivating force, in the case of these people, is generally the sex urge. And in consequence, when the novelty of physical attraction wears out, there is nothing else to hold the marriage together.

Venus rules jewels, perfumes, pastel shade in colours, and beauty of form both in human and still life.

Those who have Venus for their star of destiny will have a definite tendency to over-expression of ornamentation and depending on their resources, they are bound to have a passion for diamonds, emeralds and rubies and for symphony of colours.

Mars

Mars is a hot, dry, fiery, violent planet known as the "Bloody Planet", and performs his course in one year, three hundred and twentyone days and thirty two hours.

Mars is exalted in twentyeight degrees of Capricorn. He rules the signs Aries and Scorpio.

When this planet is nearest the earth, murders are more frequent, and are of atrocious nature. When he is retrograde, innumerable calamities and robberies take place.

37

An individual with a strong influence of Mars is strong, well set, but short, bony, lean and muscular. He has red complexion, sharp eyes and a violent countenance. Frequently a scar is found on the head or face.

When Mars is well dignified in the horoscope the native is fearless, violent, irascible and unsubmitting. Though fond of war and contention, he is at the same time pendent, rational, over generous and magnanimous.

But when Mars is ill-dignified in a horoscope, the native is inclined to violence, quarrels, treachery, robbery and many kinds of wickedness and cruelty. The native has a disposition to anger, violence, and possesses an eagerness to get into quarrels and mischief.

The native of this planet expects the universal submission, and although generous and magnanimous, he is incapable of being kind and sociable. However, these aspects may be dormant in a person, if the aspects of other planets alter the influence of Mars very materially.

Mars governs the parts of the body involving the head, face, stomach, kidneys and knees. Also the groin, bladder, organs of generation, the heart, throat and circulation.

The diseases of the planet are of an inflammatory kind, and those resulting from wounds or burns, especially affecting the face or organs of generation. Other afflictions caused by this planet are tumours, abscesses, small pox, toothache, headache, diabetes, jaundice, measles, shingles, carbuncles, hot eruptions and fevers of all kinds.

One must remember that the planet simply represents physical force, and a lot depends on the native to utilise this force in a constructive way. It can give the native vitality, courage and ambition or at the same time make him unreasonable, intolerant, impulsive, too hasty in arriving at decisions, make him take unnecessary and foolhardy risks, and give him an attitude that antagonizes those around him.

The native of this planet can be happy only when he feels that he is conquering and overcoming obstacles.

The natives of Mars are extremely sensitive people and take offense too easily.

The violent aspect of Mars not only causes fevers and sudden attacks of illness, but also it can cause gruesome accidents, because of its quick and unexpected actions. However many accidents can be avoided by maintaining the equilibrium, by keeping the temper even, and most important of all, by not becoming confused or absent-minded.

Mars sometimes interferes with accomplishments. But with reflection and visualisation preceding the action, and with caution and introspection, by the native, this can be conquered. The native of Mars must always take time to think out clearly his course of action and proceed from intelligently directed thought, and not act on impulse.

It is very essential that the native of this planet tempers his anger or resentment with mercy, and developes more sympathetic and a tolerant attitude towards the shortcomings of others. Then he will be more successful, popular and find happiness. The motto he must always bear in mind is "Counsel and patience are mightier than coercion".

Mars rules iron and sharp instruments. Therefore, the natives of Mars have the greatest aptitude in the occupations of butchers, barbers, carpenters, metal workers, soldiers, military men, surgeons, chemists and dentists

Jupiter

Jupiter is considered a hot, sanguine, airy, beneficent, masculine, social planet. He is also the author of temperance, justice and moderation. Known as the "Greater fortune" he rules over the fiery, magnetic sign Sagittarius.

Jupiter's exaltation is in fifteen degrees of Cancer.

A native born under Jupiter's influence will be tall, well built, erect, handsomely proportioned, robust, and ruddy with a commanding personality. He should have oval face, high forehead, full eyes, thick hair, wide chest, long feet and a firm and frank manner.

If the aspect of Jupiter is well dignified in a person's horoscope and he is strongly under the influence of this planet, the native will be wise, magnanimous, affable, jovial, mild in manner, temperate, just and good, and inclined towards religion and philosophy. However, the planet in its ill-dignified aspect influences the native to be conceited, indifferent, prodigal, of shallow abilities, careless, easily influenced and led astray and a fanatic in religion. He is inclined to be lazy, too dependent on luxury, and too self-indulgent.

The true character of this planet is to make his native good natured, just, a lover of freedom, and to give him a disposition that would make it uncomfortable for him to do wrong or even in contriving to do wrong. The native should, never, under any circumstances, be a bad character. His frank expression and pre-possessing appearance cause him to enjoy the confidence of others. People feel happy and secure in his society.

When an individual is lucky to have the strong influence this planet in his horoscope, his chance of success in all his undertakings in life is assured, and he receives continued help to mitigate any threatening indications from any less favourable aspects. This beneficent planet endows his native with executive ability, sound judgement and unusual vision.

One born under the dominating force of this planet will always be blessed with enough strength to bear any misfortune which may overtake him and often protect him from unforeseen dangers.

Jupiter governs the liver, lungs, the veins, blood and all the viscera. The diseases to which the native of this sign is subject are those involving those parts or which arise from plethoric habit or corrupt blood.

When the sign is afflicted at birth, particularly by Saturn, the native must take greatest care to keep the liver from being torpid and to be sure that waste substance is freely eliminated.

The sign in which Jupiter is placed and also the aspect he occupies at birth is very important as this is the source from which greatest good fortune of the native proceeds.

Jupiter being the symbol of wisdom, is the largest planet of the solar system. He is the dominating influence not only over man, but also over everything in existence. However his effect is modified by his exact position and aspects to other planets. For example, if Jupiter is in aspect to Mars, the native derives tremendous executive ability. However, if in aspect to Saturn, it has a subduing influence and restricts optimism and faith.

In general classification Jupiter may be considered the exact contrary of Saturn. Saturn constricts and conserves. Jupiter expands and spends. Jupiter is the instinct of creation, generosity, hospitality and of the spiritual emotions. He represents these qualities as bestowed upon men, and in general he is the planet who brings luck in business or profession and will contribute towards making the character of the native noble, generous and easy-going.

Venus combines well with Jupiter and if the planets are strengthened by a third planet of more robust and severe character there is a tendency to softness on the part of the native. However, the combination of the two planets Jupiter and Venus can bestow upon the native, great skill in art. But in order to deal with the stern condition in life, the stiffening effect of such a planet as Uranus, Mars, Sun or Saturn, is very essential.

Saturn

Saturn is the most distant planet from the Sun, with the exception of Uranus and Neptune. He completes his revolution in twentynine years, one hundred and sixtyseven days and five hours, and this is the duration of his year.

Saturn signifies prudence and caution. However, the aspect of Saturn, in a man implies obstacle and delay, and he exerts the force of isolation and concentration.

In general, if we consider Saturn as acting upon the man as part of his environment, he may be called unfortunate. He brings delay, and therefore makes his native despondent and hopeless. This way Saturn is the indicator of the amount of success the native may derive in life.

It is important that an individual should have favourable aspects of Saturn, and it is not good for the well being of the native to find the Saturn weak or in his detriment.

The influence of Saturn is most dominant during the first thirty years of a person's life, and after the sixtieth year—that is during the most active years of a human being's life. Saturn is the force of age and all that eats and clogs. Consequently he represents diseases which proceed from cold and obstruction, such as agues, epilepsy, toothache, black jaundice, cold defluxions, catarrh, phthisis, atrophy, melancholy, fistulas, apoplexy, dropsy and leprosy. Deafness is not uncommon with the natives of this planet. Adenoid growths, tonsilitis, diphtheria or glandular swellings upon the neck are also common ailments of the natives of this sign. Saturn's affliction in any one of the twelve signs can cause one of these illnesses.

Those born with Saturn as their planet of destiny will have much to endure and much to overcome. However, Saturn is also in a position to bestow upon his native the moral strength to overcome the obstacles and attain great rewards. The native of this sign should understand that self-sacrifice and service have to be the keynotes of their lives. Once they realise this the less they will suffer. Failure should not dishearten them and they should never give up things halfway. They should learn to battle against circumstances. No matter how thorny the path may seem, with perseverance, they may turn it into a great goal. However, if they allow themselves to be beaten in the struggle, they may fall into melancholy and take a prejudiced and bitter view of life. Only confidence and courage can continue to support them, but when this ceases, then they can be considered among those who have failed.

Patience, diligence and austerity will bring their reward to the natives of Saturn but the children of

Saturn should guard against taking life too seriously and assuming too much responsibility regarding the destiny of others. They will do well to select for partners, business associates or friends those who have an optimistic attitude towards life and are less seriously minded than themselves. With such associates they will be a greater force in the world.

The general attitude of a Saturnian is to have fewer wants than aspire for abundant wealth.

Those born strongly under Saturn must learn to cultivate patience. In life they are often likely to encounter one obstacle after another, and their success will come only after hardwork and much delay. Often they are inclined to endure difficulties rather than make a change for the fear that they may meet disappointment. Adamantly they hold on to old customs and conditions, although in some respects they are progressive and optimistic.

The Saturnians have a tendency to be sympathetic with elderly people, and the older they grow, the younger they will be in their feelings. However, they may often find it difficult to get comfort from others because of their tendency to live within themselves, although they crave for love and sympathy.

One of the strong effects of the Saturn on the natives is the tendency it gives the natives to give up at just the moment when the tide would naturally turn. And unless they overcome their timidity and self-consciousness, they will often have their feelings bent when nothing of the kind was intended. They have an inclination to magnify obstacles, and therefore they will miss opportunities and keep much good from coming to them.

When Saturn has a strong influence on the native, or the marital relations, or business partners, it tends to cause the partner to be older in years. Often the partner will tend to shirk responsibility but will expect to share equally in the profits.

When Saturn is in an elevated position of a person's horoscope, it undoubtedly causes the person to rise in life and be in a position to weild power. However, if the person is inclined to use the authority for selfish purposes, he is bound to meet with downfall. The more secure a Saturnian may seem to be at any time, the more cautious he must be to take no false step. The native must bear in mind not to disregard the best interests to those whose trust he holds. The native must avoid being too ambitious for power, and enjoy what he has, realising that no matter what he may attain he will still crave for more.

Saturn elevated deprives the native of benefits through parents and usually takes away one or both of them early in life.

A Saturnian is often self-made, man or woman, though his or her early efforts are generally attended by obstacles and delays. Usually success comes to a Saturnian only after the age of thirty.

A native of Saturn is always economical, thrifty and provident. He has a natural aversion to wastefulness and all undue extravagance.

A developed Saturnian will ever strive to succeed through his persistency, perseverance. punctuality and great attention to detail. He is never argumentative or too critical. He has learned the value of silence and wisdom of meditation. He has tremendous selfcontrol and concentration.

The undeveloped Saturnian, however, holds a very narrow outlook on life, generally, and is not above deception. He is often not unwilling to take advantage of those who are less fortunate than himself.

He is likely to meet with one misfortune after another, and he cannot escape the law of cause and effect, unless he realises that we take out of life just in proportion to what we put into it, and it pays to be honest.

The influence of Saturn is corrosive, hindering and retarding, nevertheless it is also a crystallising and constructive force when used unselfishly.

Saturnians have a strong sense of self-preservation and they may at first sight, appear self-centered but these people can be more intelligently sympathetic with pain and misfortune, because of their own unfortunate experiences, than many who are born under planets that give more noble qualities.

Saturn's good influence bestows qualities which make it possible for us to reach our highest goal. However, its malign influence tends to encourage, carelessness, indifference, suspiciousness, fear, even cowardice, melancholy and laziness. Those who are under the strong influence of Saturn should transpose this depressing influence to a higher plane. Or else they may sink to such depths and count such misfortune that they may have a very sad and lonely old age and even end their life in suicide.

Uranus

The most distant planet, with the exception of Neptune, Uranus passes through one sign of the Zodiac in about seven years and completes its circuit around the Sun in eightyfour years and twentyseven days.

A planet that has been discovered just recently, less than two centuries back, there is no record from the Ancients as to its nature or its extraordinary

46

influence on human life· Modern Astrology has however determined quite definitely its general nature and major attributes.

Uranus has its greatest influence in the sign Aquarius and stands for the interior, subconscious, magical will of persons born strongly under its influence.

The native of this planet may be in complete harmony with his surroundings at one time and feel himself as lucky, but at another time he will be entirely out of unison and consider himself as one of the unfortunate ones. Either view is, of course, illogical. However, there is no doubt that Uranus, more than any other planet, produces the most extraordinary vicissitudes. When death occurs to a native of this planet, more often than not, it is not by disease; the force of this planet is too vital and one might almost say too spectacular to bring about anything so banal. When this planet may cause death, it is usually of a catastrophic and tragic kind. For this Uranus has no equal among the planets.

Uranians are often found going in an opposite direction from the masses both in thought and action. They do not usually fall in with the crowd. By the time any fashion, custom or idea has become popular, they have outgrown it or lost interest in it.

This planet, one can easily assume is not so simple and constant in its movements as are the others. There is a peculiar uncertainty about the actions of this planet, which may be termed as tricky and unaccountable.

Uranus may be called a planet of destiny. When persons are born strongly under its influence, fate plays a large part in their existence. It gives its native an individuality which has something of the divine in it. The vibrations of Uranus transcend the ordinary dimensions of length, breadth and thickness, and go over into what may be called a fourth dimension.

Uranians are also children of opportunity, and therefore opportunism is indicated as their best strategy. Freedom is essential to these people and they cannot work in harness. They will rebel at what appears to them the stupidity of others. It is advisable for them to use the wisdom of the serpent to avoid expressing their thoughts in this respect too freely.

Uranians may appear most impractical, too readily resentful of opposition and often out of tune with the common place affairs of life. And in fact most Uranians find it difficult or even impossible to co-operate harmoniously with the average mortal.

The action of the planet can be considered most unpredictable, at one time conferring great material benefits when least expected and again causing too great independence, too great impatience, and so opposing routine or prescribed methods as to invite the opposition and misunderstandings of family and friends.

Uranians, it is very essential, learn to value the law of non-resistance and to realize that nothing happens by chance. If not they will experience most unusual happenings, suffer from estrangements and be considered by their associates as being odd or even eccentric.

The moods of this planet change very rapidly and are different at times. Therefore those born strongly under its influence may find it difficult either to be understood or to understand themselves. It is advisable that they should make the most of each opportunity and live one day at a time, forming few definite plans too far ahead. If they take this precaution it may save them much nervous strain and unnecessary disappointments.

48

This planet has the influence on mankind to advance them in the line of spiritual knowledge and to make people more impersonal and less possessive in their attitude towards life.

The influence of this planet can be reactionary, if one lives in an uncongenial atmosphere or with people who are too materialistic. Uranians penetrate and understand what appears to the ordinary individual to be impossible.

The innate character of the natives is progressive, inventive, exploring and of a humanitarian nature. The influence of the planet is the last personal, and the most universal in the Zodiac. And consequently any efforts for the betterment of humanity is favoured by those who are strongly responsive to its vibration.

The nature of this planet does not seem to favour occupations for which one gets a regular income or to help accumulate great wealth. For this reason, the natives of this planet would be well advised to make wise provision for less favourable periods. A remarkable character of this planet is that any money made during a good aspect of this planet is rarely saved. The same tide that brings it in is almost sure to carry it away. The moment the native of this planet begins to lose, it is a sure sign that the tide has changed, and, for a time, inaction is the only safe course.

Uranus stands for the higher octave of Mercury. And in order to count its most favourable vibrations, it is important that the native remains through life impersonal, unprejudiced and without ulterior motive. Only too often the force of this powerful planet becomes very destructive and malefic.

The highly developed Uranians aim at great and noble things, they are fond of philosophy and religion. They have strong intuition and possess a desire to rise above the material. Generally they are romantic, unsettled and prophetic. And they take interest in problems concerning not only personal matters, but also in national and race questions. On the whole they are extraordinary people.

The undeveloped Uranian is likely to be eccentric, abrupt and brusque in manner. He is altogether out of tune with everyday people and affairs, reckless, head-strong and even rebellious.

Uranus rules the nervous system. And therefore, when afflicted has a malign influence upon the cerebrospinal axis of a person. It often superinduces strange symptoms of a psychic character, which even a regular practitioner will find it difficult to diagnose or cure. Afflicted Uranus can also be the source of incurable organic diseases, collapse of fortune, as well as other miseries. It can also bring about headlong destruction of bad habits, misdirected affections, and illicit connections with the opposite sex. The amount of mal effects this planet can bring about depends on the signification of the place or radical affliction in the horoscope.

In order for the native to overcome the evil vibrations of Uranus it is necessary that the native should try to control appetites and passion, that he takes every step in obedience to enlighted reason and that his mind rest in the repose of an unfaltering trust in the Divine Spirit.

Where Uranus exerts a strong influence in a horoscope in the marital relations, great danger lies in the fact that Uranus gives so much individuality to the character, that it is practically impossible for either partner to merge the life in that of the other. And the effects can be very disastrous. The only safeguard would be for each partner to have a definite interest in life, leaving the other free of conventional restrictions, and develop absolutely mutual confidence.

Natives with a strong Uranian influence on the material plane, are proven to be over-confident, over ambitious and inclined to undertake hazardous schemes which may result in heavy losses. It is very essential that the natives exercise great caution and best of judgement. These people have also the habit of being very enthusiastic about a thing today, but tomorrow absolutely indifferent. This variation in the feeling is due to the influence of this strange planet. They should develop the will power to not make sudden changes or depart from legitimate activity without serious thought. Otherwise they are likely to experience strange vicissitudes of fortune and other misfortunes in their lives.

Uranus in its benevolent aspect can also bring about in the native new current of thought of a very original character, increase intuition, stimulate the telepathic faculties and elevate the mind to a higher state of consciousness. The tremendous occult force which Uranus gives, if used constructively, can make the natives powerful, in their own sphere, and make them the vehicles through which come a message to mankind.

That message may be that of art, science, literature, philosophy or religion!

Neptune

A vast, slow, and a mystical planet Neptune is the outermost planet in the Solar System and the ruler of the sign Pisces. Neptune, requires one eighth of a generation to move through a single sign. Being the planet of spirit, he is always revolutionary. Forever he increases new life, the material varying according to the signs through which he works.

Neptune, the romantic, irresponsible, that may be considered the planet of the fourth dimension, makes a revolution around the Sun in 163 years and 253 days, at a velocity of about three and one-half miles per second.

Neptune represents the forces of nature too undifferentiated to be understood by the average person. The native with a strong influence of Neptune is generally possessed of a highly organized nervous system and most acute sensibilities. He posseses a very fascinating and elusive magnetism which can exert a peculiar influence over others.

Simple and straight-forward people, who say just what they mean or mean just what they say soon bore the Neptunian. The Neptunians possess the remarkable capacity to anticipate the thoughts of others before expressed. Many a time, through this capacity, they are unable to hide their impatience, and fail to allow their companions an opportunity to finish their line of talk. This can end in confusion and likely to cause misunderstandings.

By virtue of the unusual ability they possess to visualize the complete picture, the Neptunians can foresee the outcome of events and are, rarely surprised at whatever may happen. It is very essential that they overcome their tendency to be too vague on the practical details of a plan. And they should depend on someone less creative and more objective to do this for them. Otherwise there is the risk that they will undertake impossible tasks and be accused of being imaginary or impractical.

The influence of the planet on the physical plane often manifests itself in obscure nervous troubles and heart complications. Though they may appear to be valvular, the source may be always traced to nervous or psychic. Neptunian diseases are always of an unusual kind. Sometimes they are of a slow wasting nature, and sometimes just the opposite, and under great excitement the influence of the planet can produce psycho-hysteria. Neptunians, however, possess very young arteries, that generally causes one to be older in youth and younger after middle life. They are able to see, hear and feel things which are not registered by those with less sensitive organs. In general the influence of this planet gives a love of experience.

Those born under the strong influence of this planet are usually so remote from the average individual that they may feel themselves somewhat solitary figures, among their contemporaries. In general they have a hunger for love, sympathy and happiness, but not in the same way as the ordinary person craves. They find it difficult to take life seriously.

Those with a powerful influence of Neptune in their horoscope are psychic by nature and due to the effects of the vibrations of this planet they also possess various phenomena like second sight, warning dreams, clairaudience, and clairvoyance.

One can easily spot persons born strongly under the influence of Neptune. They will always stand out in a crowd. Even at the first glance they would convey the impresssion that they are not as others. While it may be difficult to define the exact impression they convey, it is unmistakable. They appear, in some way, peculiar, highly individual, but not with any general kind of strength. They possess eyes with a peculiar magnetic quality that have an effect which is often weird and startling.

The Neptunians are often coldly penetrating, and the undeveloped types are frequently shifty and secretive, with a slight hint of perversity or madness in them.

Those born with Neptune as the dominant planet in their horoscope have very singular and subtle moral and mental characteristics. The vibrations of this planet, taking place in the remotest fastness of the soul causes deep seated upheavals of the personnality. The person often betrays a contradictoriness, a perversion, a whimsicality, or introduces some fantastic element of mockery or masquerade. In some cases this will be very profound and far reaching, and in others shallow and superficial.

In younger people Neptune can exert the influence to instil a yearning of the spirit in seeking after strange deities and frequently to the use of alcohol and drugs. More often than not Neptunians are found to possess abnormal vices.

To a Neptunian the common satisfaction of life seems too banal, and he often seeks the hidden mysteries of life. The advanced soul however realises that life is a dream, and a divine dream at that.

A Neptunian usually begins his search, inspired by a sense of dissatisfaction, and with the notion that by reversing the established order of things, which he has decided to be bad, he will attain the good. However, more often than not, he comes to the conclusion that after all things are no better one way or the other. This way he may end up gaining divine wisdom, and become content with life. While younger Neptunians possess these peculiar traits in their character, the elder Neptunians who have passed through the purifying fires, are bound to look down upon them as those who are destroying their own souls.

There is one characteristic, which is very typical of a Neptunian, which can be excessively annoying to all concerned. His mind may be perfectly made up, his judgement may be sound, and his desire unhampered but at the moment of putting his will into execution, he balks. It is not a case of being in doubt, hesitation, vacillation, a conflict of impulses, or the difficulty in striking a balance of judgement. It is pure perversity!

All Neptunians aspire to things beyond the limits of life—But the elder souls with sane minds who possess knowledge and understanding of the cosmos and have learned how to deal with passions and emotions, in them this aspiration assumes the less devastating form. Still the determination exists, but the method which appeals is carefully reasoned instead of being instinctive and is tempered by common sense, ensure that health, reason, fortune or social relations are not endangered. A person thus gifted, may show keen interest in the studies of strange philosophies and occult sciences, but he will not go astray in them. He may devote a good part of his time to prayer and meditation, but will not become a fanatic. He may adopt mystical practices which may appear weird to an average person, but he will stick to his own ideas in the matter.

While the vibrations of Neptune seem to extend from the mysterious, occult sciences to the greatest philosophies and science, the underlying impulse is always the same. Neptunians have a hunger for the infinite. The lunatic, the psychopath, the drug fiend and the saint, all are members of the same Neptunian family, but what divides them is not the result of any differentiation in the soul, but rather in the degree of knowledge and experience.

The common trait in the under-developed Neptunians, who are impractical and who possess less sense of actuality, is to pretend to be something extraordinary. It is not unusual to find some Neptunians assume titles to which they have no right. There are Neptunians who love to extra-ordinary clothes, or dab themselves with exotic strong smelling perfumes, or who make up their faces to a fantastic degree. This desire to want to pretend to be something which they are not may again express itself in other kind of actions. For example as a love of intrigue, of fooling their friends or the public, of playing practical jokes on friends or even strangers, or getting involved in situations in life, which is not natural. Better balanced Neptunians, however, will try to find expression to this tendency in a more legitimate and accepted way, like actually going on the stage.

An average Neptunian is somewhat an irresponsible person. He is very inconstant. His moral character appears weak, as it is based on mere impulse and whim, rather than on judgement, mostly inspired by self interest. Many a time he realizes that he is making himself ridiculous in the eyes of those around him, by his antics, but the selfishness of his spirit leads him to continue with them. Any hint of opposition from his family or friends will often cause him to exaggerate his errors.

Neptunians are also afflicted with wanderlust. They are usually discontented with the place where they happen to be.

A pure Neptunian type lives almost entirely in and through the psychic nervous system. His body is usually frail, delicate and petal soft, but the soul in him burns strong. This may easily wear out the bodily sheath.

When the physical functions are depressed and the nerves cannot obtain the supernormal energy which they so insistently demand, it may result in hysteria and nervous breakdown. It is not uncommon that the native whose body responds with more elasticity to the extravagance of the nervous system ends up with such incurable diseases, such as locomotor alaxia, general paralysis of the insane, softening of the brain, or other obscure afflictions of the nervous origin.

Neptunians are also vulnerable to worry and all its attendant illness.

Asterisms

The twelve signs of the Zodiac are divided into twentyseven equal parts, starting from the first point of Aries. These are called Asterisms. In the Hindu Astrology, they are known as "Nakshatras". The various planets are much influenced by the position they are placed in the Asterism.

In the Hindu system of Astrology the Asterisms in which the moon is placed at the time of birth is of great significance. The term "JANMANAKSHATRA" —Asterism of birth, is actually the position of the moon in the Asterism at the time of birth.

The Asterisms and their longitudal degrees may be tabulated as follows:

Nakshatra	Asterism	Longitude
Aswini	Beta Arietis	13°20′
Bharani	35 Arietis	26°40′
Krittika	Eta Tauri	40°
Rohini	Aldebaran	53°20′
Mrigashira	Lambda Orionis	66°40′
Ardra	Alpha Orionis	80° 0°
Punarvasu	Beta Geminorum	93°20′
Pushya	Delta Cancri	106°40′

Ashlesha	Alpha Hydroe	120° 0'
Makha	Regulus	133°20'
Purva Phalguni	Delta Leonis	146°40'
Uttara Phalguni	Beta Leonis	160° 0'
Hasta	Delta Corvi	173°20'
Chitra	Spica Virgins	186°40'
Swati	Arcturus	200° 0'
Vishakha	Alpha Libroe	213°20'
Anuradha	Delta Scorpio	226°40'
Jyeshtha	Antares	240° 0'
Mula	Lambda Scorpii	253°20'
Purva Ashada	Delta Sagittari	266°40'
Uttara Ashada	Sigma Sagittari	280° 0'
Shravana	Alpha Aquiloe	293°20'
Dhanistha	Beta Delphinum	306°40'
Shatha Bhishag	Lambda Aquarius	320° 0'
Purva Bhadrapada	Alpha Pegasi	333°20'
Uttara Bhadrapada	Gama Pegasi	346°40'
Revati	Zeta Piscum	360° 0'

The various Asterisms have definite influence on the physical and mental characteristics of the natives. It may be summarised as follows:

Ashwini

Natives of Ashwini are usually beautiful in appearance. They love to be adorned in good jewellery and clothes. They are sharp-witted, accomplished and unperturbed. Usually they have a calm temperament.

Bharani

Natives of Bharani usually have an immense zest for life. They are intellectually inclined, and have a scientific bend of mind. They enjoy good health and prosperity. They have a steady mind, and they seldom tell lies.

Krittika

Natives of Krittika have a strong physique and they enjoy good health and long life. Usually they have insatiable lust, and they are greedy in their eating habits. As a rule they are very cunning and deceitful. However they are inclined to enjoy fame and socially they move in high circles.

Rohini

Natives of Rohini usually have exceptionally large eyes. They are honest and truthful in their dealings, and generally they are generous and charitable. Talented conversationalists, they have an unperturbed mind.

Mrigashira

Natives of Mrigashira generally suffer from inferiority complex. They are persevering in nature, but love an easy way of life. Money comes to them easily.

Ardra

Natives of Ardra are usually not very trustworthy. Generally they are not very sincere. They are proud and often self-centred. They are given to quick temper.

Punarvasu

Natives of Punarvasu rarely enjoy good health. They can easily become addicted to alcohol and drugs. Though they are generally polite and tactful, when aroused, they may easily loose control over their tongues. In business dealings they are usually clever and even cunning, if necessity arises.

Pushya

Natives of Pushya usually have a calm mind. Highly intellectual, they are usually dutiful, law abiding, and righteous. They are noble in their outlook, and they are philanthropic.

Ashlesha

Natives of Ashlesha generally have a robust physique. They are of a cheerful temperament, and they have a great zest for life. However it is not unusual to find some of them insincere and cunning. Gratefulness is not a quality associated with the natives of Ashlesha.

Makha

Natives of Makha love an easy luxurious life. It is rare to find industrious people among them. They love to surround themselves with beautiful things, particularly flowers of colour and fragrance. Prosperity comes to them rather easily.

Purva Phalguni

Natives of Purva Phalguni are philanthropic minded and noble hearted. They are generally pleasant in their behaviour, and tactful in their speech. They have the knack to see ahead and therefore they make very good businessmen. However they suffer from unsteady mind.

Uttara Phalguni

Natives of Uttara Phalguni usually suffer from poor appetite. They are intellectually inclined and healthy minded. Generally, they are sincere, truthful and noble hearted, though short-tempered.

Hasta

Natives of Hasta are usually brave and chivalrous. Besides other noble qualities, they are grateful and charitable. However at times they can be merciless and stealthy. They are usually prosperous in the later part of life.

Chitra

Natives of Chitra are especially distinguished for their beautiful physique. They are noted for their shapely figure and attractive features, particularly eyes. They are fond of good clothes and ornaments. Though they can be considered good-natured in general, they are not usually sharp-witted and bright. It is not unusual to find them being stingy.

Swati

Natives of Swathi are well known for their dignified and polished manners. They are intelligent, scholarly and are able administrators. Tactful in their behaviour, they have great self-control. Dutiful and generally law abiding, they make excellent citizens.

Vishaka

Natives of Vishaka are well known for their jealousy and stingyness. They are short tempered, but at the same time they are god fearing and honest.

Anuradha

Natives of Anuradha are distinguished for their beautiful hair and eye lashes. Dutiful and god-fearing they have great attraction for the opposite sex. They will be prosperous and honoured by the great. However, natives of Anuradha will find themselves luckier in a foreign soil.

Jyeshtha

Natives of Jyeshtha have very bad tempers, giving way to violent outbursts at times. Generally they are not very prosperous, though they are charitable. They have very few friends.

Mula

Natives of Mula are very proud people. They have bad tempers and not favourably disposed towards relatives. They have a constant, steady mind and they love discipline.

Purva Ashada

Natives of Purva Ashada stand out in a crowd because of their tall stature. Generally they are proud and noble minded. Kind to people, and generous to the poor and needy, natives of Purva-Ashada are loyal friends, but dangerous enemies.

Uttara Ashada

Natives of Uttara Ashada are distinguished by their majestic appearance. Strong and muscular they usually have long nose and chisselled features. They have good discerning eyes and they are generally gentle and kind. Fond of good food and good company, they are always of a pleasant disposition.

Shravana

Natives of Shravana distinguish themselves for their high intellect and noble qualities. They are generally of polished manners and dignified behaviour. They have great enthusiasm for life.

Dhanishtha

Natives of Dhanishtha are well known for their independent nature and liberal outlook. Highly esteemed for their courage and valour, natives of Dhanishtha are also generally fond of music.

Shatha Bhishag

Natives of Shatha Bhishag possess high intellect and virtuous conduct. Always truthful and uncompromising, they are the beloved of everyone.

Purva Bhadrapada

Natives of Purva Bhadrapada are easily given to melancholy. They usually think lesser of themselves, than they are actually worth. They are intelligent and are usually gifted speakers. They easily give in to jealousy and greed. Generally they have very little faith in God.

Uttara Bhadrapada

Natives of Uttara Bhadrapada have a great aptitude for arts and science. Usually talkative they are argumentative, but tactful and diplomatic. They are generally charitable and kind.

Revati

Natives of Revati possess a perfect build and a robust constitution. They are popular, heroic, and have great attraction for the opposite sex. Tactful and diplomatic they have a wandering mind. But seldom they do anything blameworthy.

Each sign contains $2\frac{1}{4}$ asterisms. And each asterism is 13° 20″ extant.

Each asterism is sub-divided into four equal parts called "Pada". Of course each Pada is 3° 20″ extant.

When the moon is passing through certain "Pada" of some particular Asterisms at birth, the effects can be very harmful to the child, mother or the father. If, however, the evil effects are averted, through other benevolent planetary combinations, the child may

65

live upto a ripe old age, and enjoy great prosperity and glory in life.

To mention in particular, Mula 1, Ashlesha 4, Makha 1 or Jyeshtha 4 can be very dangerous to the life of the child.

How to Cast a Horoscope

A horoscope is a chart indicating the positions of the Sun, Moon, and other planets in relation to the earth and to the Zodiac for any given moment of time. Before casting the horoscope, it is of paramount importance to know the exact time of birth as accurately as possible. Even a few minutes difference may alter the entire character of the horoscope.

The year, date and time of birth, and the latitude and longitude of the place of birth, are all the necessary data, for the correct calculation of a horoscope, by the Indian method or the Western method. If we learn to cast the horoscope in the Western method, it can be easily converted to the Indian system by substracting the Ayanamsha of the year of birth from the longitudes of the houses and planets.

The two most important requisites for calculating a horoscope according to the Western system are Raphael's Ephemeris for the year of birth and the Raphael's Tables of Houses for Northern Latitudes.

In the following diagram the centre represents the earth and the outer circle the space of the heavens which is divided into twelve equal sections, called "Houses". The line that divides one house from another is known as the "Cusp". The first house begins with the horizontal line on the left side of the circle. And the Cusp of the first house is called the ascendant, as the Sun, the Moon, and other seven planets from this point on ascend, or arise and are visible in our horizon.

The sign of the Zodiac rising at a person's birth, termed the ascendant, signifies man's outward appearance and everything which has to do with the personality. Therefore the ascendant is considered one of the most important factors in diagnosing the horoscope:

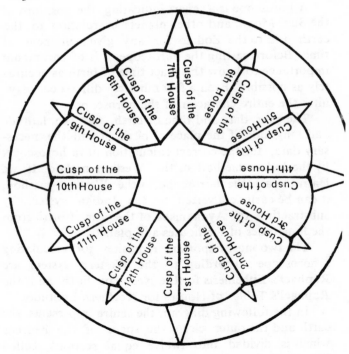

In order to erect a horoscope for any given time, two major operations are necessary. Calculations of the Cusps of different houses and calculating the positions of the planets from the Ephimeris.

Generally the time of birth of persons born in India, is recorded in terms of the Indian Standard time, which has been arbitrarily chosen for purposes of maintaining uniformity in the country and which is 5 hours 30 minutes in excess of Greenwich Mean Time. Therefore we have to convert the time of birth expressed in Indian Standard time in Local Mean Time for the place of birth. For this we subtract 5 hours 30 minutes from the IST which will give us the Greenwich Mean Time. Then we convert the Longitude of the place of birth to hours, minutes and seconds at the rate of 15° for one hour, 1′ for four minutes and 1″ for four seconds. If we add the two data, we get the Local Mean Time for the place of birth.

To simplify this calculation a table of correction for various cities in India is given at the end of this book (Table No. 1). By adding or subtracting the number of minutes and seconds quoted in the table, from the IST., one can obtain the Local Mean Time —LMT—for the place of birth.

We have now to calculate the houses for the LMT as found. We refer to the Raphael's Ephimeris and turn the pages to the required month and day. A column would be found in the left headed "Sidereal Time".

Note the Sidereal time for the day required Refer to the table No. 1 again for the correction to the Sidereal Time, to find the Sidereal Time for mean noon at the place of birth. Add the correction if the Longitude is West, and subtract if the Longitude is East.

If the birth be before noon, deduct from the Sidereal Time the difference between the Local Mean Time of birth and noon of the same day. If the birth happened afternoon, then add to the Sidereal time, the time between noon and the time of birth. In case of a birth before noon, if the Sidereal Time will not permit the deduction, then add 24 hours to it and make your subtraction. In like manner, if when adding the time of birth to the Sidereal Time, the total exceeds 24 hours, then subtract this 24 from the result, which gives the correct Sidereal Time of birth.

Having ascertained the correct Sidereal Time of birth, we turn the pages of the Table of Houses and find the table for the required Latitude. In the column marked Sidereal Time, we find the figure or the nearest thereto as the Sidereal Time of birth, we have already computed. It will be noted in this table that the figures 10, 11, 12, Ascendant, 2 and 3 occupy the top line. These represent the Cusps of the 6 houses. The remaining six houses occupy the other half of the circle, and we insert on their Cusps the same degrees of the opposite signs, and thus we complete the 12 houses.

The signs and degrees for the Cusps of the 10th, 11th, 12th, Ascendant, 2nd and the 3rd houses of the horoscope are on the same horizontal line with Sidereal Time.

As an example we shall proceed to erect a figure for the horoscope of Miss Seema Sareen, born on 24.11. 1954 at 6 P.M. IST in Calcutta:

Time of Birth in IST	—6 P.M.
Correction for IST from Table 1 as per the Place of birth	+23 minutes 30 seconds

∴Local Mean Time	— 6 hours
	23 minutes
	30 seconds

Sidereal Time on 24.11.1954
Mean Noon (Greenwich)   —16 hours
                                 11 minutes
(By Referring to the   38 seconds
Ephimeris)
Correction to Sidereal Time
for Mean Noon at Place of
Birth   —58 Seconds
(By Referring to Table 1)

∴Sidereal Time at Mean Noon at the Place of Birth—16 hours 11 minutes 38 seconds—58 seconds=16 hours 10 minutes 40 seconds.

The Difference Between Mean Noon and the Time of Birth Expressed in LMT—6 hours 23 minutes 30 seconds

The Time of Birth being P.M.	16.10.40
We add the Correct L.M.T.	+6.23.30
to the Sidereal Time at Place	————————
of Birth at Mean Noon	
Sidereal Time of Birth	=22.34.10

Now we set about to find the houses:

We turn the pages of the table of houses for the Latitude 22°33′ N (Calcutta). We find the nearest Sidereal time to our Sidereal time of birth to be 22 hours 34 minutes and 54 seconds, which gives us 7 degrees of Pisces on the Cusp of the 10th house, 10° of Aries on the eleventh house; 16 degrees Taurus on the 12th; 19° 46 minutes of Gemini on the Ist or Ascendant; 14 degrees of Cancer on the Cusp of the second; and 9 degrees of Leo on the 3rd. We fill in the remaining six Cusps with the same number of degrees, but with the opposite signs. Our Cusps are now complete and the map should now look as below:

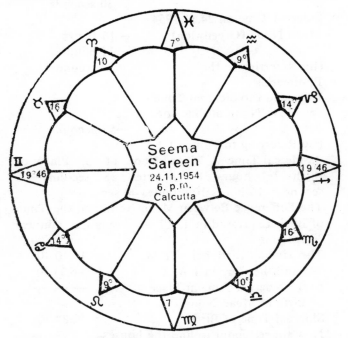

Now we proceed to insert the planets in the houses:

We refer to November 24th in the Ephimeris. In the column headed "Long" (Abbreviation for Longitude signifying the planets' position in Zodiac) and under the planetary symbols, we find the planets' positions expressed in degrees and minutes; and seconds in the case of Sun and the Moon. Of course, it is understood that each sign of the Zodiac contains 30 degrees, each degree 60 minutes and each minute 60 seconds. When the seconds exceed 30, it may be taken

72

to the next higher minute and if under thirty, it can be omitted.

The planet's places given in the Ephimeris are calculated for noon at Greenwich and therefore we must change the IST to Greenwich Time. This is done by subtracting 5 hours and 30 minutes from the IST. We now subtract 5 hours and 30 minutes from the IST of birth 6 P.M., which gives us 12:30 PM. This subtracted from noon, upon which all calculations in the Ephimeris are based, gives 30 minutes for which period the movement of Sun, Moon and the other planets, is to be calculated.

The Sun's Position

The position of the Sun has to be calculated for 12:30 PM GMT. By referring to the Ephimeris we find that the Sun's longitude on 28th November 1954 was 1°40'30" of Sagittarius.

On the 23rd of November 1954, the Sun's longitude was 0°39'49".

∴In one day Sun's motion was—

1°40'30"—0°39'3"=1°00'51"

We can take this as approximately 1°1'0"

(The daily motion of planets for all the days in the year can also be found in the pages 26—28 of Raphael's Ephimeris)

Sun's motion in 24 hours—1°1'0"

∴Sun's motion in 30 minutes or

$\frac{1}{2}$ hour — $\frac{1°1'0"}{24} \times \frac{1}{2} = 1'12"$

(This can also be found by the use of proportional logarithms contained in the last page of the Raphael's Ephimeris. The method of using it can be learnt therefrom)

Having calculated the Sun's motion in 30 minutes we add it to the Sun's position at noon, the birth being afternoon:

$$1°40'30'' + 0°1'12'' = 1°41'32''$$

The Sun's position at birth = 1°41'32" in Sagittarius.

The Moon's Position

The motion of the Moon is more erratic varying from about 12 degrees to 15 degrees in 24 hours. We note from the Ephimeris that the position of the Moon was 20°36'55" in Scorpio on the 24.11.1954. On the next day, that is, 25.11.1954 the moon is found in 2°27'24" of Sagittarius.

Therefore the Moon's motion in one day

$$32°27'34'' - 20°36'55'' = 11°59'39''$$

Moon's motion in 30 minutes or ½ hour =

$$\frac{11°50'39''}{24} \times \frac{1}{2} = 15 \text{ approximately.}$$

Moon's position at birth 20°36'55" + 0°15'0" = 20°52' in Scorpio

The Other Planets

In the same manner as above the positions of the planets Mars, Venus and Mercury can be found. But Neptune, Uranus, Saturn and Jupiter being slow

74

moving planets, their positions may be inserted in the map as found in the Ephimeris.

In cases where a planet is close to the end or the beginning of a sign, it is more necessary to ascertain its exact position and it should be accurately calculated.

The planets are moving, not only at various rates, but because of the relative motion of the earth in the ecliptic at certain periods in any year they appear to be moving backwards. At such time they are said to be "Retrogarde". This is signified by the symbol "℞". The Sun and Moon, of course, are never Retrograde.

Having found the exact position of longitudes of the Sun, Moon and the various other planets, we tabulate them as follows:

	Planet	Longitude
☉	Sun	1°41′32″
☾	Moon	20°51′55″ or 20°52″
♆	Neptune	27°5′
♅	Uranus	27°30′
♄	Saturn	14°24′
♃	Jupiter	29°51′
♂	Mars	23°4′
♀	Venus	17°19′
☿	Mercury	15°12′

We now proceed to insert these planets in their proper houses on the horoscope.

The first house, or the ascendant is in the position of 9 o'clock on the face of a watch or clock. In order that the planets may rise, the signs on the Cusps of the houses must move backwards. This comes from the fact that it is the earth that moves on its axis, causing the sun to appear to rise, as in reality the heavenly bodies remain practically stationary for the twentyfour hours. Therefore, the planets go with the clock, and the signs rise in the opposite direction.

Referring to the diagram 1, which shows the position of the heavens or the twelve houses, on the 24th of November 1954 at 6 P.M. and the degrees of the Zodiac on the Cusp of each house, we will proceed to place the planets in the diagram 2.

We found that the moon after being corrected was in 20° Scorpio 52 minutes and as Scorpio 16° is on the Cusp of the sixth house, we must place the moon in the sixth house. We found that the Sun, after being corrected was in 1° Sagittarius 41 minutes and as 19° Sagittarius 46′ is on the Cusp of the 7th house, we must place the Sun below the line of the 7th house, that is the sixth house. Neptune being 26°, Libra 5 minutes will occupy the 5th house as 10° Libra is on the cusp. Uranus being in 27° Cancer 30′ will be placed in the 2nd house as 14° of Cancer is on the Cusp of the 2nd house. Saturn being in 14° Scorpio 24 minutes will be in the 5th house, below the line of the cusp of the 6th house Scorpio 16°. Jupiter being 29° Cancer 51′ will be placed in the 2nd house as 14° Cancer is on the cusp. Mars being in 23° Aquarius 4′ will be placed in the 9th house as 9° Aquarius falls on the cusp. Venus being in 17° Scorpio 19′ will be in the 6th house as 16° of Scorpio is on the cusp. Mercury being in 15° Scorpio 11′ will fall in the 5th house.

The diagram below illustrates the complete horoscope of Miss Seema Sareen, born on 24th November 1954 at 6P.M. IST in Calcutta:

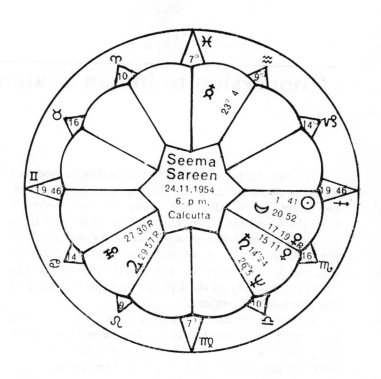

Conversion to Indian System

The horoscope according to the Indian method can be easily deduced from the previous calculations, with two simple steps. All that we have to do is to subtract from the longitude of the cusp of Ascendant and from the Longitudes of the planets, the "Ayanamsha" of the year of birth. Ayanamsha is the "Precession of Equinoxes" and may be found referred to as the "Mean Obliquity of the Ecliptic" on the first page of the Raphael's Ephimeris.

An important factor to be taken into account while converting the horoscope to the Indian method is that the planets Neptune and Uranus are not given cognizance in the Indian Astrology, perhaps because they have been discovered by Western Astronomers comparatively lately.

Rahu and Ketu play an important role in the Indian Astrology. However, it must be mentioned here that Rahu Kethu are not exactly planets, though for the purposes of prediction, in view of their obvious effects on human affairs, they are considered as such in Indian Astrology. They are in fact the Ascending and Descending nodes of the moon, the places where the moon, in its orbit cuts the celestial equator. The nodes are called the tail and head of the dragon. Rahu, the dragon's head is represented by the symbol ℛ," and Ketu the dragon's tail is represented thus ℧,

Let us now proceed to convert the horoscope of Seema Sareen to the Indian system:

Ayanamsha for the year 1954—23°27'. This has to be subtracted from the longitude of cusps as well as those of planets.

Signs

10th House	7°—23°27'	=	13°33'
11th House	10°—23°27'	=	16°33'
12th House	16—23°27'	=	22°33'
Ascendant	19°46'—23°27'	=	26°19'
2nd House	14°—23°27'	=	20°33'

Signs

3rd House	9°—23°27'	=	25°33'
4th House	7°—23°27'	=	13°33'
5th House	10°—23°27'	=	16°33'
6th House	16°—23°27'	=	22°33'
7th House	19°46'—23°27'	=	26°19'
8th House	14°—23°27'	=	20°33'
9th House	9°—23°27'	=	25°33'

Planets

Sun's Long	1°41′—23°27′	=	8°14′
Moon's Long	20°52′—23°27′	=	27°25′
Saturn's Long	14°24′—23°27′	=	20°57′
Jupiter's Long.	29°51′—23°27′	=	6°24′
Mars' Long	23°4′—23°27′	=	29°37′
Venus' Long	17°19′—23°27′	=	23°52′
Mercury's Long	15°12′—23°27′	=	21°45′
Rahu	7°24′—23°27′	=	13°57′
(From the Ephimeris)			
Ketu		=	13°57′

The figures secured from the above calculations should be inserted in the chart as in the following diagram:

		Lagna	Ketu
			Jupiter R
Mars			
Rahu	Sun	Moon Saturn VenusR Mercury	

This chart is known as the Nirayana chart.

The house in which the Lagna or the Ascendant is placed is the "Janma Lagna".

In this case the Janma Lagna is "Vrishaba".

The house occupied by the moon is the "Janma Rashi".

In this case the Janma Rashi is Tula

And the Janma Nakshatra is found by referring to the table of "Nakshatra Divisions" and "Vimshottari Dasa" (Table No. 2) given at the end of this book. We take the number of degrees occupied by moon in a particular house, and by comparing it with the table we secure the exact Janma Nakshatra.

In this case the Janma Nakshatra is "Vishaka"

Navamsa Kundali

The Rasikundali is only a sketch of the positions of the planets, and to get a greater precision of the positions of the Cusps and planets there is a system of more accurate form of recording these positions, in the Indian Astrology. This is called the "Navamsa" Kundali. In this method every sign is divided into 9 equal parts and each part has the rulership of the particular planet who rules over the complete sign in the natural order.

For example Aries (Mesha) is divided into 9 equal parts, the first part, that is upto 3° 20′ is ruled by the ruler of Mesha—Mars. And the second part, that is upto 6° 40′ is ruled by the ruler of Vrishabha, which is Venus, so on and so forth.

Therefore in order to place a particular planet in a particular house we have to find in which of the 108 divisions each longitude falls, and following that order, we have to place the planet or cusps of the Ascendant in the different signs.

The table of Navamsa is given at the end of this book (Table No. 3).

Here is the completed Navamsa Kundali of Seema Sareen's Horoscope:

Lagna Saturn	Mercury	Venus	Moon
Ketu			
			Rahu
			Jupiter Mars Sun

The Rising Signs

The sign that is rising, in other words the ascendant, or the Lagna in Jndian Astrology, and the sign in which the ruler is placed at a person's birth, determines his physical appearance, more than any other factor. However, where the ruler of the rising sign is weak or afflicted, the position of the sun or of the moon, in male or female nativities respectively, are more important.

There is the possibility of modifications of practically all characteristics of any rising sign, when there happens to be a planet in cl6se proximity to the Ascendant. Let us take for example the general notion of a Leo born, whose face, we imagine is of a ruddy complexion and frank expression. Saturn or Uranus rising will have a positive influence on his complexion. Saturn will darken his complexion and might lengthen his face and give an expression of gravity and more resolute.

It may be assumed, however, that generally speaking the planets have a far more positive influence than the signs of the Zodiac. It would be quite difficult to get an absolutely pure example of the unmodified action of any sign, since its ruler is always somewhere in the heavens, varied in diverse ways, by his position. Therefore, we may safely presume that the Zodiacal sign is of the nature of an atmosphere rather than a unit of force.

This may seem somewhat imperceptible but on keen observation one would easily find that the signs of the Zodiac are more recognizable at a glance than any planetary combination.

The general characteristics of the Ascendant, or the rising sign, will be, of course, most modified when a powerful planet of an opposite nature occupies the sign. For example let us take the sign Cancer. In this sign there are two main types. The passive, watery and Luna type and the aggressive, cardinal Jupiter type. Supposing Mars and Uranus are rising in conjunction in this sign, naturally, they will almost wipe out the former, while emphasising the latter. However, it must be remembered that, while such elements of confusion must be taken into account, no combination of planets, however powerful, can wholly destroy the general effect of the rising sign. For example, no possible modification of Scorpio can give the effect of Libra. The characteristics or temperament of the individual will remain the same, though in the background. One may slow up the action of Scorpio in various ways, but the result is to produce hesitation in the execution of rash action, not to prevent the original hasty resolution. We may safely assume that the signs of the Zodiac divide humanity into twelve major classes— immaterial of the race, nationality or religion.

It would seem as if I am trying to convince my reader that Astrology is so simple as to suppose that the infinite variety of face and figure which humanity presents, is to be classified in so rough and ready a fashion. No. Every degree has its own peculiar magical image. And the difficulties connected with the measurement of time are enormous. And this is usually an inaccuracy of at least a few minutes in the casual observation taken of a nativity. It is only through patient experience one can distinguish the finer and finer vibrations.

The infinite variety in the details of complexion, feature, physical proportions, which all contribute towards the appearance of an individual depends to a considerable extent upon other factors than the Zodiac. A great deal depends on the modifications caused by rising planets or by the rule of the Ascendant sign. Every planet contributes its work. For example Mars rules the muscular system. Supposing we have a general type inclined to femininity, softness or fatness, the robustness will depend upon Mars and be modified by his strength or weakness by position or aspect. Let us assume that Venus is rising in Pisces. That will determine the general appearance. But if Mars should be in Capricorn, the muscular system, particularly in the lower parts of the body, will be lean and strong. Almost like that of steel and whipcord.

It is important to remember that every planet possesses multiple functions. Mercury, for example, rules the conscious mind. But his position and aspects will also determine the appearance of the mouth, as well as all those parts of the body that are ruled by him.

While describing the personal characteristics from a nativity, it is important to consider every detail separately and then form a judgement as to its probable effect in modifying the main type. The overall welfare of a being depends on the harmony of all the elements of his make up, and a single point in his disfavour is likely to ruin the rest of the structure. A beautiful body like that of Adonis is not much good if the head happens to be hydrocephalic. Likewise, a man may possess all the qualities of a great statesman, but if he should be a hopeless alchoholic, these qualities will have no chance to operate.

Therefore, it is very necessary in every case to work out with minute accuracy the power of each planet in each degree and to gain a thorough knowledge of the limits within which aspects become operative.

Nevertheless, it is also necessary to bear in mind that whatever may be the planetary influences in the horoscope, they never really outweigh the general type of the Zodiacal sign rising.

Planetary Aspects

In the Western system of Astrology planetary influences work through "Aspects". An Aspect is the distance which separates one planet with another, or with any point or the horoscope. All planets can aspect all other planets. But we take into account only the aspects formed by well defined angles. There are two kinds of aspects, the benefic, harmonious ones or the malefic, unharmonious ones. They can be grouped as follows:

The Benefic Aspects

Semi Sextile
   Connects one or several planets by an angle of 30°. Slightly good.

Sextile
   Connects one or several planets by an angle of 60°. Good.

Trine
   Connects one or several planets by an angle of 120°. Very good.

Quintile

Connects one or several planets by an angle of 72°. Slightly good.

B₁ Quintile

Connects one or several planets by an angle of 144°. Slightly good.

The Malefic Aspects

Semi Square

Connects one or several planets by an angle of 45°. Slightly bad.

Square

Connects one or several planets by an angle of 90°. Bad.

Sesqui Quadrate

Connects one or several planets by the angle of 135°. Slightly bad.

Quincunx

Connects one or several planets by an angle of 150°. Slightly bad.

The opposition

Connects one or several planets by an angle of 180°. The planets being opposed, their qualities are not able to be manifested freely. Very bad.

(In Hindu Astrology this aspect is however considered good).

These aspects are called malefic or unharmonious, because the connecting planets are positioned within the Zodiac signs with which they have no affinity at all.

Now there are two other aspects that are important The Parallel symbolised as "P" and conjunction with the symbol "♂" The conjunction which has no angle at all can be beneficial, if the coupled planets are of a similar nature such as:

Moon	—	Jupiter
Venus	—	Jupiter
Venus	—	Moon
Sun	—	Jupiter
Sun	—	Venus

The conjunction is malefic, when the nature of the united planets don't agree. For example:

Saturn	—	Mars
Sun	—	Mars
Uranus	—	Mars

The parallel, however, is of a different nature. In the Ephimeris there is a column with the heading "Declination", which is measured by the South or North of the celestial equator, in terms of Latitude when the two planets are equidistant on either side of the celestial equator, then they are said to be situated in the same degree of declination. Immaterial of their degrees in longitude, they attract or aspect one another, and this aspect is known as the "Parallel" aspect represented by the symbol "P". The effect of "P" is similar to that of conjunction "♂"

Of the various benefic and malefic aspects the most powerful ones are the Trine and the opposition. And the other aspects fall in this descending order of importance:

P ▢ ✳ ⊡ < ⋎ Q B♂

90

Speculum

The horoscope is not complete without a table of aspects formed by the different planets in the horoscope. And this is called "Speculum". In order to calculate the speculum, we have to consider the planets one by one, and count how many degrees each is apart from the others. The distances then calculated, if they correspond to any of the aspects are said to be formed.

However the difference in longitudes of planets may not be necessarily 30°, 45°, 60°, 90° or 120°. They may vary by a few degrees. Therefore a margin of 7° is always allowed on both sides. This margin of 7° is generally known as the "ORB" of influence.

Let us now compute the speculum of Miss Seema Sareen's horoscope.

Taking the planets in their order, it is found that the aspects as shown below are formed:

♅	☌	♃	2½°	(Applying)
☿	☌	♄	¾°	(Separating)
☿	☌	♀	2°	(Applying)
♀	☌	☽	3½°	(Separating)
☽	□	♂	2°	(Applying)
♅	□	♆	½	(Applying)
♆	□	♃	2½	(Applying)

Bhavas

In the Indian system of Astrology, besides the effects of signs and planets, the house positions have also been taken into consideration. These houses are known as the Bhavas.

It is already known that there are twelve houses comprised by the twelve signs. The Sun remains in one sign for about a month in the horoscopes of all persons born during a month. And while in that sign he exerts an influence peculiar to his tenanting that particular sign.

Various planets, including the Sun and the Moon make different angles with the Eastern horizon as viewed from the place of birth. And this angle determines the house position of a planet.

Each house represents some part of the human body, relations, friends, financial positions and other departments of life. And to diagnose a horoscope we have to take into consideration the planet owning the house and the planets occupying or aspecting the house.

When different signs rise in the eastern horizon, the subsequent signs comprise subsequent houses. Thus if Libra is the rising sign, Capricorn constitutes the 4th house. Similarly if Leo is the rising sign, the fifth house will be Sagittarius. Then Jupiter, the ruler of Sagittarius will be the lord of the fifth house.

The Sun and the Moon are the lords of one house each, as they own one sign each, but Mars, Mercury, Jupiter, Venus and Saturn are the lords of two houses each, because each of them own two signs.

Rahu and Ketu never become the lords of any house as they do not own any sign.

The house positions may be grouped as follows:

Angles (KENDRA) : The first, fourth, seventh and the tenth house are known as angles. Planets herein are deemed to have great influence on the native in bringing him power and fame.

Trines (TRIKONA) : The first, fifth and ninth houses are known as Trines. Planets in Trines are also considered good and powerful.

Succedents (PHANAPARA) : The second, fifth, eighth and the eleventh houses are known as Succeedents houses. Planets herein are considered weak and they bring about indirect results.

Cadents (APOKLIBAS) : The third, sixth, ninth and the twelfth houses are known as cadents. The planets herein are considered weak, and to some extent malefic, mainly affecting the mental side.

All the departments of a man's life, health, wealth intelligence, misery, happiness, friends, enemies, relations, trade and commerce travels etc. come under some house or the other.

According to the Indian system, certain planets have certain aspects, which are very good. They are as follows:

Sun	in the 7th House
Moon	in the 7th House
Mars	in the 4th, 7th and the 8th house
Mercury	in the 7th house
Jupiter	in the 5th, 7th and the 9th house
Venus	in the 7th house
Saturn	in the 3rd, 7th and 10th house
Rahu	in the 7th house
Ketu	in the 7th house

These aspects are considered to apply to the whole house, and of course they are neither good or bad on their own, but depend upon the planets in relation to one another, and to the horoscope.

In the earlier chapters of the book, we have already discussed characteristics of the various planets in detail, and their influence on the natives.

Yogas

Planets placed in certain particular positions which have remarkable effects on the natives are called the "YOGA". Some of the special Yogas are described below:

Raja Yoga

When the lords of the Ninth house and Tenth house are situated in one another's house or are in conjunction with each other in either of the above houses, they produce "Raja Yoga"—good luck in all undertakings.

Kesari Yoga

When moon is in "Kendra" position to Jupiter, the effects produce "Kesari Yoga", and the native is blessed with a keen intellect, and a capacity to speak in large assemblies. He will occupy high position and amass fame.

Lakshmi Yoga

When Venus and the lord of the Ninth house is in 5th, 9th or in position of "Kendra" and at the same time in his own place, "LAKSHMI YOGA" is produced. The native will be blessed with a luxurious life, happy family, health, wealth and all the other comforts of life.

Saraswathi Yoga

Venus, Jupiter and. Mercury in the position of Kendra or Trikona or in the 2nd house while Jupiter occupies his own house, the effect ·produced is "Saraswathi Yoga". The native will be blessed with a keen intellect, and wisdom. He will be a scholar, good in poetry and mathematics. He will also amass wealth and enjoy a happy family life.

Ruchaka Yoga

When Mars occupies his own place and in the aspect of trine to the lagna, the native will enjoy the effects of Ruchaka Yoga. He will be blessed with wealth, fame and victory.

Hamsa Yoga

When Jupiter is placed in his own house and in the aspect of trine to the lagna the effect is "Hamsa Yoga". The native will enjoy great prominence in society, admiration, and a commandeering position. He will be envied even by his enemies. He will possess a beautiful body and a charitable mind.

Bhadra Yoga

When Mercury is placed in his own house, and is in the aspect. of trine to the Lagna, the effects are Bhadra Yoga. The native will enjoy long life, keen intellect, wealth and prominence in society. He will be a good speaker in the assemblies.

Malava Yoga

When Venus is placed in his own house and is in the aspect of trine to the lagna, effect is Malava Yoga. The native is blessed with great wealth, enormous property, large family, posh vehicles, servants and keen intellect.

Vallaki Yoga

All the seven planets, if they occupy one house each, beginning from Lagna, consecutively, Vallaki Yoga is effected. The native will be very talented in music, dancing and fine arts.

Sasaka Yoga

When Jupiter occupies his own house and is in the aspect of trine to the lagna, Sasaka Yoga is effected. The native will be blessed with great wealth and all comforts in life. But he will be a person of easy virtue.

Dhama Yoga

When all the seven planets occupy signs consecutively from the Lagna, Dhama Yoga, is effected. The native will be a very philanthropic minded person.

Chamara Yoga

When a beneficial planet occupies the Lagna, which is well aspected, and the lord of the Lagna is also well aspected, Chamara Yoga, is effected. This is a highly desirable Yoga. The native will be blessed with long life, great wealth and fame.

Dharidra Yoga

When the lord of the 11th house in 6th, 8th, 12th or 16th is occupied or aspected by malefic planets, Dharidra Yoga takes effect. The native will be poor, devoid of comforts in life, subservient to others, and possess awkward and uncouth behaviour.

Chakata Yoga

When moon is in the 6th, 8th or 12 th house from Jupiter, Chakata Yoga is effected. The native will experience misfortunes and various disappointments in life.

Khemudra Yoga

When there are no benevolent planets in or on either side of the Lagna, or in the moon's place, or in their Kendras, then the Khemudra Yoga is effected. The native will live in poverty, though born rich, and lead an undesirable type of a life.

Rajju Yoga

When all the planets in a horoscope occupy the movable signs, Rajju Yoga is effected. The native will be famous, enjoy interrupted fortunes.

How to Judge a Horoscope?

While judging a horoscope, one has to collect all the relevant information revealed by planetary positions, go from house to house, and draw conclusions, taking into consideration the environment of the native.

The first point one must consider in a horoscope is whether the native will live long or not. This is decided by the nature of the rising sign, the lord of the rising sign, the condition of the various planets rising, the nature of Sun, Moon and the lord of the eighth house. If the Moon, Sun and the lord of the eighth house are strong, the native will enjoy a long life. However, the result will be the opposite when the positions are as follows:

(1) Jupiter, Uranus or Mars is near the rising degree and is afflicted by the ruler of the 8th house. And without any beneficial aspects from Jupiter or Venus.

(2) When the Sun, Moon and the lord of the ascendant are afflicted.

(3) When the birth takes place during the course of an eclipse.

The physical description of the native is usually decided by taking into consideration the rising sign, planets aspecting the ascendant, the signs they occupy and also most important of all the ruler of the ascendant.

Bodily defects in the native can be traced, if the planets combine as follows:

(1) Capricorn, Aquarius or Pisces rising and the malefic planets afflicting the rising degree.

(2) Sun and Moon afflicted in Capricorn, Aquarius or Pisces.

(3) Where a malefic planet is situated and badly aspected, in a particular house, defects in that part of the body can be predicted.

(4) When Mercury is in the 12th house or is the lord of the 12th house and is afflicted by Mars, Jupiter, Sun or Uranus or when the house corresponding to the ear and its lord is afflicted, deafness in the native can be predicted.

(5) When Uranus occupies the sixth house and Mercury is afflicted the native will suffer a chronic ailment, incurable.

(6) When Sun or Moon is in Aquarius and is afflicted by Jupiter or Mars by conjunction or opposition, blindness in the native can be predicted. However, in the case of Moon, cure, can be hoped for.

(7) When Mercury or Venus is very near the Sun, defects in the eye of the native can be predicted.

(8) When Mercury afflicted by Jupiter occupies Cancer, Scorpio or Pisces, the native will stammer.

The financial situation of the native is indicated by the moon and planets in the second house and tenth house, in the horoscope of men and sun, instead of moon, in the horoscope of women. Mars in the second house, badly aspected by Venus indicates financial losses caused by overspending on personal luxury. However Saturn in a similar position signifies calculated economy and wise spending. But a badly aspected Saturn in the same position can also mean stinginess and greed.

The fifth house indicates the love life, children or speculation of the native. A badly aspected Venus in this house, in a woman's horoscope indicates a hectic love life. If Uranus or Neptune should rule the house or even be present in this house and is afflicted, it indicates perversion.

If, in the seventh house, moon is badly aspected, it signifies, sudden changes. However, if it is badly aspected by Mars, it signifies separation. When it is afflicted by Jupiter it signifies divorce.

When the planet in the fifth house rules the second house, or vice versa, the native will be very lucky in lotteries, races, or other kinds of gambling.

If in a male's horoscope, the Mars forms an angle with the Venus of a female horoscope, this indicates strong physical attraction. Reciprocity of the Sun and the Moon in the first and seventh between the horoscopes of a man and a woman indicates strong affinity between them.

Any affliction in the cusp of the sixth house or the eighth house by Mars, Uranus or any other planet occupying the ascendant afflicted signifies accident. If Sun and Moon are connected with this affliction, the accident will be a serious one. The sign from which the malefic influence proceeds, will decide the part of the body that will be injured.

The tenth house is considered the house of occupation, but the root of occupation is decided by the

101

first house. Saturn placed in the tenth house signifies, changes for the better and rise in the latter half of the life. Mars placed in a similar position indicates rise in life through one's own effort. Jupiter in the tenth house indicates that the native will excel in Law or allied subjects, and may hold a senior official position. Uranus in this position denotes that the native will be a successful rebel, and also excel in electricity, invention of mechanical gadgets and things of similar nature.

A strong second house and a well aspected Mercury indicates a successful businessman. And a strong connection between Venus and other planets indicate a successful artist.

A powerful Mars or Uranus in a horoscope indicates a successful engineer or artisan, and a powerful Jupiter indicates a successful politician.

The combination of a bad Mercury and Neptune denotes criminal inclinations in the native. Mars in bad aspect with Neptune or Saturn indicates the native to possess inclinations to murder, and if the combination is involved in the fifth house, the native will also possess inclinations to murder, rape and other sex crimes.

In the Indian method of Astrology, however, while the main principles of judging a horoscope is pretty much the same, it differs in the respect, that the houses are taken one by one, and are examined in all their aspects for the nature of the house, nature of its lord, nature of the lord of the house, influence of other planets upon it, and also the state of the particular planet called "karaka"— meaning the significator — who has a special connection with the specific matter under consideration.

According to the Western as well as the Indian systems of Astrology, each planet holds a particular portfolio in their aspects on human life, immaterial of the Lagnas or other variable factors in a horoscope. Here is an enumeration of the Karakas and their charge:

Sun	:	Represents the soul . Stands for father, wealth, fame and power.
Moon	:	Represents the heart, as well the emotions connected with the heart. Stands for mother.
Mars	:	Represents the stamina and the prowess. Stands for brothers and sisters, husband, accidents, courage and weapons.
Mercury	:	Represents speech and intelligence. Stands for maternal uncle, nephew, education and trade.
Jupiter	:	Represents sons and daughters. Stands for learning and wisdom, honours and priesthood.
Venus	:	Represents wife or husband. Stands for worldly comforts, romance, art, jewels and conveyances.
Saturn	:	Represents servants. Stands for sorrow, hard work, unpleasantness, poverty and longevity.
Uranus	:	Represents electricity.
Neptune	:	Represents psychology.
Rahu	:	Represents spiritual attainments, stands for paternal grand father, poison and pilgrimage.
Ketu	:	Represents maternal grand father. Stands for Leprosy.

Kendra, Panapara and Apokliba houses are very important in the Indian system of Astrology. Benefic planets in these positions indicate a happy childhood, middle and old ages respectively. They also signify good yogas. However, when malefic planets occupy the same positions. misery could be predicted.

Several planets occupying exaltations, own houses, trines or angles, and also strong Jupiter, Venus or Mercury indicate a prosperous life. So does a well placed and a well aspected moon.

If the lord of the ninth house is strong or exalted, or occupies the first, third or the ninth house, then a glorious life can be predicted for the native.

One should always consider the Bhavas or the houses with reference to Lagna, the Moon and the Karaka. This process will make the judging of a horoscope much easier.

Lords of the fifth and ninth houses may be always considered benevolent, whereas the lords of the third sixth and the eleventh houses may be considered malefic. However, if the malefics are the lords of the Kendra houses or trines will do good, and vice versa, if benefics are lords of Kendra, they will only have evil effects. Jupiter and Venus may be mentioned in particular. However, lords of the second and the twelfth houses are greatly influenced by the aspects of other planets.

With the exception of the Sun and the Moon, lord of the eighth house can be considered malefic, unless he is lord of the Lagna. When he is the lord of the Lagna, of course, he will do good.

The lords of the Kendra and Trikona, when associated can do a lot of good, though independently they may be harmful to the native.

Here is an analysis of the various combinations of the planets with reference to each of the twelve Bhavas.

Before we go on to tabulate the various planets in their order of qualities, an explanation of two important terms used in Indian Astrology, will be necessary.

The term "Yoga Karaka" signifies a planet that becomes the lord of an angle as well as a trine. It becomes totally good auspicious to the native, and during its period, causes very many changes for the better in the life of the native.

"Maraka" is another important term in astrology and it signifies the evil influence of the planet which may bring death to the native.

Now we shall proceed on to tabulate the effects on the planets in the various Bhavas in the following order :

Lagna	Malefics	Benefics	Yoga Karakas	Marakas
Mesha	Saturn Mercury Venus	Jupiter Sun		Saturn Mercury Venus
Vrishabha	Jupiter Venus Moon	Saturn Sun	Saturn	Jupiter Venus Moon
Mithuna	Mars Jupiter Sun	Venus		Mars Jupiter Sun
Karkata	Venus Mercury	Mars Jupiter	Mars	Sun Venus Mercury

105

Simha	Mercury Venus	Mars		Mercury. Venus
Kanya	Mars Jupiter Moon	Venus	Venus Mercury	Mars Jupiter Moon
Thula	Jupiter Sun Mars	Saturn Mercury	Moon Mercury	Jupiter Sun
Vrischika	Mercury Mars Venus	Moon	Sun Moon	Mercury Mars Venus
Dhanu	Venus	Mars Sun	Sun Mercury	Saturn Venus
Makara	Mars Jupiter Moon	Venus Mercury	Venus	Mars Jupiter Moon
Kumbha	Jupiter Moon Mars	Venus	Mars	Moon Mars
Meena	Saturn Venus Sun Mercury	Mars Moon	Mars Jupiter	Saturn Venus Sun Mercury

To gain a thorough picture of a horoscope, one should study each of the twelve Bhavas in all their bearings, and then a synthetic analysis should be made. Each Bhava should be treated as the Lagna and checked for its strength and weakness and the sum total of the study would apply to the whole horoscope.

The Bhavas which contain the Benefic planets Venus, Mercury or Jupiter, or have their aspects without being deprived by the combination or aspects of other planets will signify a very good life for the native. This same rule applies for the Lagna as well as all the other eleven houses. And at the same time if the lords of the various houses—Bhavas—are similarly aspected or combined by the above mentioned benefics, unaspected and not joined by others, the Bhavas become even more powerful.

When the Bhavas contain weak planets lords of the eighth and the twelfth houses will be very much weakened. And the Bhavas occupied by own friendly planets will thrive.

Lords of the Bhavas occupying 6th, 8th or 12th houses or Neecha or weak planets occupying Bhavas are detrimental to the Bhavas. However, if they are aspected by the benefics, the opposite will be the effect.

Lords of the Bhavas occupying Kendra or Trikona positions, and aspected by benefics or their occupying exalted, or own a friendly position will strengthen the Bhavas.

Those horoscopes with Bhavas whose trines and angles are occupied by benefics and not occupied or aspected by malefics, nor containing the lords of 6th, 8th and 12th houses, all kinds of prosperity can be predicted for the native. If the position is reverse, of course, the opposite will be the result. Mixed, will mean mixed results.

When the Sun occupies the 8th, lord of the said Bhava be combust and no benefic lord of the 8th is joined, complete destruction of the Bhava can be predicted. The lords of Bhavas included with the lord of the 8th house indicates the destruction of the Bhavas.

The lord of the Bhava, if he occupies 6th, 8th or the 12th house position or be weak or in enemy's house, then the planet occupying the Bhava, no matter how strong, is incapacitated of correcting the situation. A similar situation in the Navamsa Kundali will also effect the same result. However, if lords of the Bhavas occupy exalted, or own a friendly house in the Navamsa Kundali, although ill-placed in the Lagna Kundali, or they be aspected by benefics in the Navamsa Kundali, then those Bhavas are progressively productive of good results.

Navamsa Kundali plays a very important role in the evaluation of a horoscope, as can be seen from the above two rules, and therefore it is very necessary to chart out an accurate Navasmsa Kundali in every case, and no attempt should be made to predict the events, without reference to it.

While surmising the strength of the Bhavas in a horoscope, the important considerations are as follows:

(1) Assuming that the lord of the Bhava is strong by his position, for example he is tenanting a friend's house, whether he is so in the Lagna Kundali, or the Navamsa Kundali.

(2) Whether the friend, whose house he is tenanting happens to be weak or strong. If he is weak, then the original Bhava also becomes very weak.

(3) If the dispositors are strong by exalted positions, or in friends or own places, then the original Bhavas, though weak by themselves, become strong.

A Bhava is considered to be strong, when friends of its lord, his exalted lord, the planet to which that Bhava is exalted occupy 11th, 2nd or 3rd places. However, if these planets are weak, combust, or the enemies to the houses, the opposite will be the result. Here again one must bear in mind the following three points:

(1) The strength of a Bhava is proportionate to its Navamsa.

(2) Malefic influences, predominating on the Bhavas will destroy them.

(3) If the lord of the Lagna has a good aspect to a particular Bhava, this will mean auspicious results. But then if a malefic planet happens to be lord of the Bhava and aspects the same, the result will be the opposite.

The nature of a house indication can be predicted only from the nature of the influence that house receives. Suppose we are evaluating the first house, an aspect to this house from the lord of the 6th house will mean trouble through enemies; aspect of the lord of the 12th house means poverty; and aspect of the lord of the 8th house, will mean danger to life.

Opposite indications of two different planets do not mean that they destroy each other. Each will have its own individual effect.

However, when a planet has the rulership of two houses, there is the unusual situation of the planet bestowing to conflicting effects on a single Bhava. In such a case, the stronger of the two will prevail.

To decide the question of direction with reference to a Bhava one of these points have to be taken into consideration:

   (1) The planet aspecting it
   (2) Lord of Bhava
   (3) Planet tenanting it
   (4) The Navamsa of the lord of the Bhava
   (5) The Navamsa of the Bhava Karaka

A **Bhava** becomes effective when the lord of the **Lagna or the** lord of the Bhava, Karaka, Planet or Jupiter transits, the Bhava or the houses occupied by the lord of the Bhava either in the Rasi Kundali, or in the Navamsa Kundali or their trines. And when the lord of the eighth house transits any of the above houses the Bhava may be considered defective.

If a planet transits through the Lagna, or the place tenanted by the lord of the Lagna, effects will be the same as indicated by the original horoscope, as being due to the planet.

Now we shall consider each important aspect of human life and the factors in the horoscope that contribute to these aspects:

Longevity

Malefic planets on both sides of the Lagna, and the house which Moon occupies; Moon in the 6th or 8th house, with the aspect of malefic planets; waning moon in 8th house and malefics in angles and trines; moon in Lagna, with Saturn, Rahu or Mars occupying the 8th house—all these factors in a horoscope, effect, a very short life to the native, unless they are mitigated by the beneficial rays from Jupiter.

If the lord of the Lagna is strong, lord of the eighth house is strong, Moon is strong, lords of Lagna, eighth house and sun are on friendly terms; Saturn unafflicted, unafflicted Lagna, eighth house and tenth house; lord of Lagna is exaltation and aspected by Jupiter, with the lord of the eighth house strong—then the native is assured of a long life.

110

Marriage

The seventh house indicates marriage. Hence this house must be free from affliction for a happy marriage. Its lord, and the lord of the house it tenants and Venus for a woman and Mars for a man must be strong and free from affliction.

If Sun occupies the seventh house in the Rasi Kundali, and the house of Mars in the Navamsa Kundali; Lords of second and seventh house, or Venus in the sixth, eighth or twelfth house is afflicted; Venus is tucked in between two malefics; or malefics are situated in second, fourth or eighth house from that of Venus—the married life will not be a happy one.

The number of planets in the seventh house determine the number of wives a man will marry. The malefics tenanting the seventh house indicate death for the wife.

The native will enjoy a happy married life if:

The lord of the seventh house together with Sun, Moon, Mercury, Venus or Mars occupies the sixth, eighth or the twelfth house.

One can predict the Lagna of the girl a man will marry, and also the direction of the native place of the girl.

A man will marry a girl with her Lagna either the fifth or ninth house, from the house tenanted by the lord of the man's Lagna or his seventh house, or the houses of exaltation of the lords of the first or the seventh house in the man's horoscope

Between the lord of the seventh house and the planet tenanting the seventh house and Venus, we must ascertain which is the most powerful. The direction indicated by the house owned by that planet will point the direction of the birth place of the girl.

The timing of the event of the marriage in a man's life can be fixed by the following method:

(1) When Jupiter transits the house tenanted by the lord of the seventh house, either in the Rasi Kundali or the Navamsa Kundali.

(2) When Venus or the lord of the seventh house transits the house tenanted by the lord of the first house either in the Rasi Kundali, Navamsa Kundali or their trines.

Agreement of Horoscopes

Among the Hindus, it is customary to consult the astrologer regarding the matching of the boy's and girl's horoscope, before their marriage is fixed. The rules of finding the agreement of the horoscopes, are as follows:

(1) The Nakshatras from the girl's to that of the boy must be counted. The total should be divided by nine. If the remainder is 4, 6 or 9, this will indicate that the horoscopes are best matched, assuring the couple a long and happy married life. If the remainder is 1, 2 or 8 the matching is tolerably good. But if the remainder is any other number, the matching is altogether unfavourable.

(2) The number of nakshatras counted from the girl's to the boy's, if it be 4, 7, 10, 13, 16, 19 or 25, one may safely assume that the couple will be blessed with a number of children.

(3) If the nakshatras counted from the girl's to the boy's exceeds 13, it indicates that the couple will enjoy great wealth.

(4) The lords of the Lagnas or the lords of the houses in which the moon is situated in both the horoscopes should be friendly. If not, at least equals. Or if a particular planet happens to be the lord in both the horoscopes, a very happy married life can be predicted for the couple.

(5) If Mars is tenanting 2nd, 4th,7th, 8th and 12th houses counted from Janma Lagna, Moon or Venus it is harmful to the life of the partner, unless it is balanced equally in the other person's horoscope.

(6) The Janma Rasi of one of the partners, if it be the 7th from that of the other, the marriage will be a very happy one.

(7) On the other hand if the boy's, Janma Rasi is 6th from the girl's, the marriage life will be full of quarrels.

(8) If Mars is afflicted in the horoscope of the boy as well as the girl, the marriage will be a very auspicious one. However, if one is afflicted and the other not, the marriage will be a disaster.

(9) When Mars tenants Aries, Cancer, Scorpio or Capricorn in either the 4th or the 7th house, he loses all his venom and becomes a benefic.

(10) Jupiter, in his benefic aspect helps a lot to nullify the evil effects of the malefic Mars.

Children

The children are judged from the fifth house, ninth house, their lords and Jupiter. Malefics occupying or aspecting the fifth or the ninth houses cause sickness to the children, or even destroy them.

If the lord of the fifth house Moon and Venus, tenant even signs both in the Rasi Kundali and the Navamsa Kundali, the children will be all girls. On the other hand if the lord of the fifth is male and tenants the odd sign in both the Rasi Kundali and Navamsa Kundali, the children will be all boys.

If the lords of the first and fifth, or the first and ninth mutually aspect each other, or are friends, or are conjoined, the general relationship between the native and his children will be a good one. However, if the lords of the first and fifth or the first and ninth are enemies and are in sixth and eighth from each other there will be no cordial relationship between the native and his children.

The number of houses between the places occupied by the lord of the fifth house in the Rasi Kundali, and the Navamsa Kundali indicate the number of children the native is destined to have.

The fifth or the ninth house from Lagna or from the house occupied by Moon or Jupiter if it be tenanted by a malefic, without any redeeming features, to counteract the effect, the native will be childless.

Education

For education one must look into the fourth and the fifth houses and their lords. Jupiter is a Karaka for wisdom and Mercury is a Karaka for intelligence. These two planets must be considered in detail along with the planets tenanting the fourth and fifth houses and aspecting them.

A strong Mercury, and absence of affliction to this planet will signify high intellectual accomplishments for the native.

Profession

The tenth house will determine a man's profession. We must consider carefully the nature of the tenth house, the nature of its lord, the nature of planet or planets, tenanting the tenth house and the aspects they receive from other planets. The house tenanted by moon at birth also plays an important role in judging a man's profession. Therefore the tenth house from the house occupied by the moon must be also considered carefully. The professions that may be followed by the native's will be indicated by the various combinations of signs and planets as follows:

(1) If one of the signs, Aries, Leo or Sagittarius is in the tenth house then the native will follow the medical profession, or be a military man.

(2) If one of the signs Taurus, Virgo or Capricorn is in the tenth house then the native may follow the line of Agriculture, farming, shopkeeping or other trades.

(3) If one of the signs Gemini, Libra or Aquarius is in the tenth house, then the native may be a mathematician, technician, public speaker, politician or a scientist.

(4) If one of the signs Cancer, Scorpio or Pisces is in the tenth house then the native may take up the line of catering, inn keeping, dealing in liquors, fishmongering, navigating, nursing, or allied professions.

The native with the Sun in exalted position will be an officer of the Government, or a top executive in a firm. He may also hold a prominent position in a world-wide organisation.

Moon in an exalted position will mean that the native may take up the line of trading in grocery, jewellery, precious gems like Diamond, Sapphire, rubies, and pearls, or precious metal like gold and silver. He may also be a sailor, hydroengineer, or a hospital worker.

Mars in an exalted position will produce doctors, surgeons, soldiers, policemen, butchers, employees in armament factories, or distinguished sportsmen.

Mercury in an exalted position produces intellectuals like writers, artists, poets, mathematicians or astronomists.

Jupiter has influence over philosophers, priests, religious leaders, judges, lawyers, ministers, professors and statesman.

Venus produces mainly artists of various kinds like poets, musicians, painters, dancers, actors and interior decorators.

Saturn has influence over labourers, miners, occultists, magicians, blacksmiths, and pot makers. But then there is one redeeming feature. If however, Saturn is placed in the tenth house, the native will be blessed with highest honours.

Rahu and Ketu have no portfolio of their own. However they stand in for other planets.

Wealth

Jupiter is the significator of wealth. The second, ninth and the eleventh houses govern financial matters. If these houses and their lords are powerful, the native will be blessed with much money. Jupiter and moon in the second, ninth or the eleventh house and the lords of the houses, in exalted positions, will mean great wealth to the native.

However, it must be noted that the effect of Saturn in the second, ninth or the eleventh houses is unfavourable. The combination of the planets Mars and Venus produces very desirable aspects and confers great wealth on the native.

Property

The fourth house, stands for the immovable property the native might own. If the lord of the first house comes together with the lord of the fourth house—in the fourth house—the native will suddenly acquire immovable properties.

Conveyances

The type of vehicle a man may possess or not possess at all will be judged from the fourth house. Venus in the fourth house mean that the native will possess excellent vehicles.

End of Life

The manner in which a man will die is judged from the eighth house The factors to be considered are the planet tenanting the eighth house, aspects received by the eighth house, and the navamsa tenanted by the lord of the eighth house.

Various planets may cause death in different ways. Their influences in bringing the life of man to an end are as follows:

Sun : Fever, stomach ailments, lethal weapon, accidents, particularly caused by fire

Moon : Bodily disorders, small pox, tuberculosis.

Mars : Black magic, murder, fire or haemorrhage.

Mercury : Delirium, insanity, meningitis, anaemia.

Jupiter : Sudden death by heart attack.

Venus : Sexual diseases.

Saturn : Typhoid, worms, gastric trouble, ulcer.

Rahu : Small pox, poison, leprosy or other incurable disease.

Ketu : Accidents connected with water, suicide.

When the lord of the eighth house, or the eighth house itself occupies the various signs, death will be caused by different kind of maladies. They can be listed as follows:

Aries : Fever, indigestion, gastric troubles.

Taurus : Inflammation of the lungs, throat troubles, lethal weapons.

Gemini : Stomach ulcers, diseases connected with the lungs, kidney failure.

Cancer : Meningitis, gastric troubles, liver or kidney disorders.

Leo : Dog bite, or other animal bite, fever, boils, drugs, attack by enemies.

Virgo : Diseases connected with sex, fall from height.

Libra : Fever, typhoid, malaria, meningitis or other diseases of the brain.

Scorpio : Dysentry, anaemia, diphtheria, liver and kidney disorders.

Sagittarius: Lethal weapons, accidents connected with water, fall from height.

Capricorn : Diseases connected with the brain.

Aquarius : Ailments of the heart, consumption, fever, asthma, delirium.

Pisces : Elephantiasis, too much water in the body, accidents in water.

Dasa

Dasa system is a very important part of Indian Astrology. Events are timed by the planetary periods called "Dasas" and transits called "Gocharas".

The Dasa system divides a man's life into periods, sub-periods, and minor sub-periods, which are characterized by the various planets. Moon is the starting point in life. It is believed by the seers of Hindu Astrology that moon exercised the greatest influence over man's life.

There are two main varieties of Dasas, the "ASHTOTTARI DASA" and "VIMSHOTTARI DASA". In this book we shall deal with the Vimshottari Dasa only, which is more popular and considered to be more correct.

As per Vimshottari Dasa the life time of man is 120 years and this period is divided among planets in the following manner:

Sun's Period	—	6 years
Moon's Period	—	10 years
Mars' Period	—	7 years
Rahu's Period	—	18 years
Jupiter's Period	—	16 years
Saturn's Period	—	19 years
Mercury's Period	---	17 years
Ketu's Period	—	7 years
Venus' Period	—	20 years
TOTAL	—	120 years

These are the major periods for which the planets hold sway and they follow a fixed order.

In order to find the Dasa at the time of a person's birth, we first of all have to find out the "Nakshatra" at the time of birth. "Nakshatras" are actually zodiacal divisions in angular distance of 13°20″ each, and they are a convenient order of calculating the longitudes of planets. Each Nakshatra is named after a lord, and a fixed point Mesha coincides with "Krittika" Nakshatra. The Sun is the acknowledged lord of "Krittika" Nakshatra. The Nakshatras follow the order Sun, Moon, Mars, Rahu, Jupiter, Saturn, Mercury, Ketu and Venus respectively as their lords, immediately following Krittika.

The angular distance of each Nakshatra being 13°20″, the full life cycle of 120 years is covered by the nine periods—giving us 13°20″ x 9 = 120° or one-third of the passage of moon over the full Zodiac. Therefore, by the time the moon has covered 120 degrees the life cycle of 120 years can be assumed to have come to an end. On this basis, the progressing of the moon by one degree, has been equated to one year of life.

The Nakshatra of birth known as "Janma Nakshatra"— the constellation in which the moon is situated at birth – can be easily ascertained from the table of Nakshatra divisions – Table No. 2 given at the end of this book. And the same table also gives the opening Dasa.

In order to calculate the dasa as well as the balance dasa period, at the time of a person's birth, all we have to do is to refer to the Raphael's Ephimeris and calculate the longitude of moon, from the time of birth, subtract from it the Ayanamsa of the year of birth, and having secured the exact position of the moon according to the Indian system, by referring to the table of Nakshatra divisions, we ascertain the exact Nakshatra at birth. And from the same table we know the opening Dasa. Now the only thing remaining for us to find is the balance of the Dasa period outstanding at the time of birth. There is a very simple method of finding this out.

We already know that the measure of a Nakshatra is 13°20″. This being the case the total number of years of the opening dasa is equated to 13°20″. Therefore it goes without saying that the portion of the years that are proportionate to the degrees yet to be covered by the moon, in order to complete the balance degrees in the Nakshatra, will be the outstanding years of the opening Dasa. Once we have found the opening Dasa, and balance period left in the opening Dasa, the other Dasas will follow a fixed order

As an example we assume that moon has travelled 7°44″ in Revathi Nakshatra. A table of Dasa allotments (Table No. 3) is given at the end of this book. Referring to the table to Dasa Allotments it is seen that the opening Dasa of Revathi is Mercury and the duration of Mercury is 17 years. In order to find out how much of Mercury Dasa is outstanding at the time of birth, we follow the simple steps as given below:

The total measure of Nakshatra = 13°20' subtracting 7°44' from 13°20'

we get — 13°20'—6°40'=6°40'

$$13°20' = 17 \text{ years}$$

$$\therefore \quad 6°40' = \frac{6°40' \times 17 \text{ years}}{13°20'}$$

$$= 8 \text{ years and 6 months}$$

The balance period of Mercury Dasa at birth is 8 years and 6 months.

To eliminate this calculation a table of Dasa balances is given at the end of this book. (Table No. 4).

After the Mercury Dasa Ketu follows for 7 years. Ketu is then followed by Venus for 20 years, Sun, for 6 years, Moon for 10 years, Mars for 7 years, Rahu 18 years, Jupiter 16 years and Saturn 19 years

In order to find the sub-periods one has to refer to the table of Dasas (Table No. 4) given at the end of this book.

Dasas and their Effects

In general the Dasas of planets who are the lords of the angles or trines, have very benevolent effects on the native. The Dasas of the lords of the second, third and the eleventh houses, produce mixed effects and the Dasas of the sixth, eighth and the twelfth houses unless mitigated by other favourable factors, produce harmful effects. However, the Sun and the Moon are exceptions to this rule in respect of the eighth house rulership only. The effects of the lords of the various houses during the period of their rule on the life of the native may be grouped as below:

Lord of the First House   —   The native will be surrounded by relatives and well wishers.

Lord of the Second House   —   The native will be setting up a family, and home life will be a happy one.

Lord of the Third House   —   Results are unfavourable. Failures and disappointments.

Lord of the Fourth House	—	Acquisition of proper-ties and other assets.
Lord of the Fifth House	—	Child birth
Lord of the Sixth House	—	Danger from enemies
Lord of the Seventh House	—	Marriage
Lord of the Eighth House	—	Recovery from illness
Lord of the Ninth House	—	Profit in various under-takings.
Lord of the Tenth House	—	Good luck in specula-tion
Lord of the Eleventh House	—	Gains in various enter-prises.
Lord of the Twelfth House	—	Illness, expenditure, mental worries.

These effects magnify when the lords are strong. During the major Dasa of a planet, its own sub-period will be of not much significance.

During the periods of "Yoga Karakas", a table of which has been given in an earlier chapter, the male-fics are incapable of effecting their evil influence. And, of course, during the major Dasa of a malefic planet the sub-period of a good planet, which is not influenced by the ruling planet, is incapable of effecting good results. However, those that are influenced effect mixed results.

The highly benign effects of a planet that produces Raja Yoga, show themselves in the sub-period of the "Maraka"—Killing—planet, during the major Dasa of the former. And the benevolent effects go on increasing in the sub-periods of malefic planets during the same major period.

The major Dasas of those planets that are the lords of the third, fifth or the seventh Nakshatras, counted from the birth star, are also malefic.

Generally speaking, the favourable planets begin to give out their good effects when the Sun or Jupiter bring in their sub-periods in the major Dasa of the former.

The various influences that will prevail during the periods of rule of the different planets may be set out as follows:

Sun : When he is strong, in his major period or minor period, is capable of bestowing upon the native wealth, fame, happiness, well being of family, betterment of general living conditions, conquest of enemies, and other benefits.

When he is adverse, by his position or aspect, the results will be sickness in the family, sorrow, danger to the life of father or mother, extravagance, fear from enemies, disappointments in job and other misfortunes.

Moon : In his good aspect he bestows upon the native prosperity, health, well being of father and mother, increase in assets, happiness in family life, success in intellectual pursuits and other blessings.

In his adverse aspect however, he brings sorrow, ill-health to mother and father, loss of money, loss of assets, ill-health and even death.

Mars : In his favourable aspect Mars confers upon his native, during his rulership, riches, clothes and ornaments, profits in business, fulfilment of desires, and general happiness.

In his adverse aspect however he turns the native into a man of loose morals, a thief, blackmailer, and one who is disliked by everybody.

Mercury : During the rulership of Mercury, in his good aspect, he confers upon the native a sharp intellect and scholarship. The native will pursue literary activities and receive acclaim.

Mercury in his unfavourable aspect can cause the native to become dull and thick headed.

Jupiter : In his beneficial aspect he confers upon the native the highest honours and a most glorious life.

In his adverse aspect he can be very evil. He causes loss of money and friends, disgrace in society, ill-health to members of the family and other misfortunes.

Venus : In his favourable aspect he bestows upon the native great artistic achievements, happy marital relations, birth of son, gains in business and high social recognition.

When adverse, he can bring upon the native ill-health, expenses and other displeasures.

Saturn : During his rulership, in his benevolent aspect, he offers the native various gains, leadership in society, excellent health and strength and a scholarship of occult studies.

But in his adverse aspect he can bring upon the native untold misery. The native will suffer notoriety, bondage, imprisonment, debts, madness, slander, poverty and all kinds of other misfortunes.

Rahu : In his good aspect he can confer upon the native, during his rulership, marriage, birth of a son, wealth, expansion of landed properties, devotion to God, and other benefits.

An adverse Rahu will mean, ill-health in family, disappointments in the various pursuits, loss of health and even death due to poisoning.

Ketu : During his rulership, in his favourable aspect, he can confer upon the native riches, power, domestic happiness and other benefits.

A bad Ketu will mean frustrations and failures, death of close friends, loss of assets by theft, and other unforeseen troubles.

Transits

While the influences of the planetary periods and
sub-periods are of major importance in arriving at an
accurate analysis of the horoscope, "Transits" are
also important to predict the future events. "Transit"
in Astrology means the passing of a planet through
a particular part of the Zodiac—in other words
through particular sign. The birth chart, or the
horoscope is fixed one, giving us the location of the
planets as they were at the time of birth. However,
the planets are not stationary, and they are always
going round in their orbits. Therefore, when we consider effect of transits, we actually take into account,
where in their respective passages, the various planets
are in the heavens, at a particular part of the native's
life for which transits are being considered.

The method of transit in the Indian System of
Astrology is known as "Gochara".

The house of the moon at birth is taken as the first
house, and the transits of the various planets is calculated from that starting point. In Indian Astrology
the moon sign is commonly referred to as "Janma
Rashi", while in the Western System, it is known as
the "Radical Moon". And the positions of the various

planets at the time of transit are known as the "Transiting Sun", "Transiting Moon", "Transiting Mercury" and so on, in the Indian system of Astrology as well as the Western system of Astrology.

Suppose a person has the moon in Gemini in the horoscope at the time of birth, and on the day he consults the Astrologer the Moon is in Sagittarius, then we say that the transiting moon is the seventh from the Janma Rashi.

When a particular planet transits some places from the Janma Rashi, and if another planet is transiting a sensitive area, the effects of the former's transit are obstructed. These sensitive areas—obstructing places—are known as "Vedha" in Sanskrit.

The effects of the transits of the planets in the twelve different houses, counted from the Janma Rashi at birth, may be grouped as follows:

Sun's Transit

First House : Illness, sorrow, decline of prosperity, changes for the worse

Second House : Decline in income, disappointments, diseases connected with the eye or head.

Third House : Good health, increase in income, promotion in job.

Fourth House : Loss of health, general unhappiness in the family, delay in undertakings.

Fifth House : Ill health, worries, persecution.

Sixth House : Increased income, contentment, improvement in general living con-

129

		ditions, good health, success in all undertakings.
Seventh House	:	Financial problems, illness, sudden changes.
Eighth House	:	Sorrow, Illness, accidents, misunderstandings, stomach troubles.
Ninth House	:	Ill health, frustrations, worries, danger from enemies.
Tenth House	:	Success in undertakings, friendship of great men and women.
Eleventh House	:	Profits in business, good luck in gambling, good health and honour.
Twelfth House	:	Fever, worries and frustration, unnecessary wandering.

Vedha places of Sun are: 3 and 9, 6 and 12, 10 and 4 and 11 and 5.

There is no Vedha between the Sun and Saturn as Sun is considered the father of Saturn in the Astrological Mythology of the Hindus.

Moon Transit

The moon completes one orbit in 27 days. In other words he covers all the 12 signs in 27 days. Therefore, he is in each sign for approximately 2 days and 6 hours. The transits of moon has to be judged in terms of the sign he is passing through as counted from the Janma Rashi.

First House	:	Sound sleep, good food, gain of good clothes and ornaments.
Second House	:	Unforeseen obstacles in undertakings, heavy expenditure, criticism from friends.

Third House	:	Good health, success in all undertakings, unforeseen profits.
Fourth House	:	Mental worries, unprofitable wandering.
Fifth House	:	Disappointments, worries, sorrow, ill-health.
Sixth House	:	Profits in business, success in all undertakings, good health, happiness in home life.
Seventh House	:	Unforeseen luck, general happiness.
Eighth House	:	Insomnia, worries, ill-health, losses in various ways, quarrels with friends.
Ninth House	:	Fear from enemies, anxiety.
Tenth House	:	Profits, success in undertakings.
Eleventh House	:	Unexpected guests.
Twelfth House	:	Heavy expenditure, anxiety.

Vedha places of Moon are:
1 and 5, 3 and 9, 6 and 12, 7 and 12, 10 and 4, 11 and 8

There is no Vedha place between Moon and Mercury.

Mars' Transit

First House	:	Fever, unnecessary travels, fear from enemies, anxieties.
Second House	·	Obstacles, criticisms, heavy expenditure

131

Third House	:	Success in all undertakings, profits, good health
Fourth House	:	Aimless wandering, worries, ill-health.
Fifth House	:	Ill-health, anxieties, disappointments, sorrow
Sixth House	:	Happiness in home life, increase in assets, good health.
Seventh House	:	Profits, general happiness.
Eighth House	:	Ill-health, insomnia, worries, losses.
Ninth House	:	Danger from enemies.
Tenth House	:	Profits, success in all undertakings.
Eleventh House	:	General happiness, success.
Twelfth House	:	Heavy expenses, quarrels, criticisms.

Mercury's Transit

First House	:	Failure in examination, unhappy home life, forgetfulness.
Second House	:	Increase in assets, unforeseen gains, good food, recognition of talents.
Third House	:	Fear from foes, unhappy surroundings
Fourth House	:	General happiness in home life, increase in income
Fifth House	:	Quarrels with relatives, mental depression, sorrow.

132

Sixth House	:	Success in all undertakings, gains through literary activities.
Seventh House	:	Separation from family members and beloved ones, quarrels, general exhaustion.
Eighth House	:	Success in all undertakings, general happiness.
Ninth House	:	Quarrels with relatives, worries, ill-health.
Tenth House	:	Increase in income, promotion in job, good health.
Eleventh House	:	Profits in business, unforeseen luck. Happiness in family life.
Twelfth House	:	Quarrels, illness, anxiety, humiliation.

Vedha places of Mercury are: 2 and 5, 4 and 3, 6 and 9, 8 and 1, 10 and 7, 11 and 12

Jupiter's Transit

First House	:	Loss of position, anxiety, changes for the worse.
Second House	:	Happiness in home life, gains from unexpected sources, success in undertakings.
Third House	:	Danger from enemies.
Fourth House	:	Death of close friends or relatives, heavy expenditure, general unhappiness.
Fifth House	:	Great success in intellectual pursuits, honours, promotion in job, gains of clothes and jewels, increase in assets.

133

Sixth House	:	Losses, ill-health, anxiety.
Seventh House	:	Ill-health, mental worries.
Eighth House	:	Illness in the family, unexpected tragedies, bondage, imprisonment, slander, unnecessary wanderings.
Ninth House	:	Popularity, recognition of services, acts of charity.
Tenth House	:	Losses, humiliation, obstacles.
Eleventh House	:	Promotion increase in income, unexpected gains.
Twelfth House	:	Separation from spouse, heavy expenditure, despondency.

Vedha places of Jupiter are:
2 and 12, 5 and 4, 7 and 3, 9 and 10, 11 and 18

Venus' Transit

First House	:	Good food, sound sleep, comforts.
Second House	:	Happiness in home life, increase in profits, honour.
Third House	:	Unexpected gains, general happiness.
Fourth House	:	Changes for the better, improvement in living conditions, honour of relatives, pleasant journeys.
Fifth House	:	Happy home life, well being of family members.
Sixth House	:	Illness to spouse, humiliations, anxiety.

Seventh House	:	Quarrels with the opposite sex, tension, worries, minor illnesses.
Eighth House	:	Expansion of landed properties, gains from unexpected sources, enjoyment with the opposite sex.
Ninth House	:	Romance, profits, philanthropic activities.
Tenth House	:	Disappointments, quarrels, humiliation, anxiety.
Eleventh House	:	Happiness in home life, unexpected gains.
Twelfth House	:	Gains in clothes and ornaments, perfumes, luxurious surroundings.

Vedha places of Venus are:
1 and 8, 2 and 7, 3 and 1, 4 and 10,
5 and 9, 8 and 5, 9 and 11, 11 and,6 12 and 13

Saturn's Transit

First House	:	Illness to the spouse, children and relations, fear from enemies, petty quarrels, bad food, worries
Second House	:	Ill-health, losses, unnecessary wandering, quarrels, general unhappiness.
Third House	:	Success in undertakings, gains, recognition of talents, happy events, good news.
Fourth House	:	Ill-health in family, sorrow, worries.

Fifth House	:	Losses of money and friends, insults, humiliation, illness, quarrels
Sixth House	:	Success in all undertakings, defeat of enemies, unexpected profits, good news.
Seventh House	:	Separation from the spouse, journey, heavy expenses, minor illness.
Eighth House	:	Litigation, public scandal, death of near relatives, general unhappiness.
Ninth House	:	Decline in income, losses, misunderstandings.
Tenth House	:	Illness, humiliation, unnecessary wanderings.
Eleventh House	:	Recognition of merits, gains of riches, good news, expansion of assets.
Twelfth House	:	Sorrow, heavy expenditure, accidents.

Vedha places of Saturn are:
3 and 12, 6 and 9, 11 and 5.
There is no Vedha between Saturn and Sun.

The transits of Rahu and Ketu will weild the same influence as those of Mars and Saturn with the difference that the Sun does not act as an obstructing force in case of Saturn, but does so in case of Rahu and Ketu. And it must also be noted that as Rahu and Ketu · are always seventh from each other. So Rahu does not act as an obstructing factor for Ketu and vice versa.

136

Sun and Mars will usher in their effects as soon as they enter the houses, while Jupiter and Venus, halfway in the houses, Saturn at the time of leaving the houses, and Moon and Mercury throughout their sojourn.

The guidelines of the effects provided above will be tempered by the strength or weakness by position, rulership and aspect of their planets. For example, besides the Vedha position, an aspect between a good and bad planet counterbalances the effects of both, whereas the bad aspect, of two bad planets will multiply the bad effects. Naturally, the good effects of a weak planet will be weak. However, the Moon just becomes the enhancer of the good or bad effects indicated by the various planets with which it conjoins during its temporary stay in the different houses.

Transit system should be always considered with the Dasa system, checking one with the other. And it should be borne in mind that however benevolent a planet may be in its blessings, during its transit, the Dasa system also should lend itself to be taken advantage of. And also, while coming to the final analysis by this method, the value of all the planets in the various houses should be taken into account, and their net effect alone should be considered.

It is also essential to bear in mind that no two horoscopes are identical. Only the relative strengths of the various planets and special aptitudes in respect of individual horoscopes should be taken into account. And each reading should be individualised.

TABLE 1
Table of Correction for Various Cities
And
Correction to Sidereal Time

Cities	North Latitude	East Longitude	Correction To I. S. T		Correction To Sidereal Time	
			Min	Sec	Min	Sec
1	2	3	4		5	
Agra	27° 11'	78° 2'	—17	52	—0	51
Ahmedabad	23° 2'	72° 36'	—39	36	—0	48
Ajmer	26° 27'	74° 38'	—31	28	—0	49
Aligarh	27° 54'	78° 4'	—17	44	—0	51
Allahabad	25° 28'	81° 52'	—2	32	—0	54
Amaraoti	20° 56'	77° 45'	—19	0	—0	51
Amarkot	25° 21'	69° 4'	—53	44	—0	45
Ambala	30° 23'	76° 46'	—22	56	—0	50
Amritsar	31° 38'	74° 53'	—30	28	—0	49
Asansol	23° 42'	86° 58'	+17	52	—0	57
Aurangabad	19° 52'	75° 18	—28	48	—0	49
Bangalore	12° 58'	77° 36'	—19	36	—0	51
Bankura	23° 14'	87° 4'	+18	16	—0	57
Bareilly	28° 21'	79° 23'	—12	28	—0	52
Baroda	22° 18'	73° 13'	—37	8	—0	48

138

Place	Latitude	Longitude				
Bellary	15° 10'	76° 56'	—22	16	—0	51
Bharatpur	27° 13'	77° 29'	—20	4	—0	51
Bhatinda	30° 12'	74° 56'	—30	16	—0	49
Bhilai	21° 12'	81° 24'	—4	24	—0	53
Bhopal	23° 16'	77° 25'	—20	20	—0	51
Bhubaneswar	20° 15'	85° 50'	+13	20	—0	56
Bhuj	23° 16'	69° 48'	—50	43	—0	46
Bijapur	16° 51'	75° 44'	—27	4	—0	50
Bikaner	28° 1'	73° 19'	—36	44	—0	48
Bilaspur (M. P.)	22° 5'	82° 8'	—1	28	—0	54
Bombay	18° 58'	72° 50'	—38	40	—0	48
Burdwan	23° 15'	87° 54'	+21	36	—0	58
Calcutta	22° 35'	88° 23'	+23	30	—0	58
Calicut (Kozhikode)	11° 16'	75° 48'	—26	48	—0	50
Cannanore	11° 52'	75° 21'	—28	36	—0	50
Cape Comorin	8° 6'	77° 34'	—19	44	—0	51
Chandernagore	22° 52'	88° 22'	+23	28	—0	58
Chandigarh	30° 44'	76° 53'	—22	28	—0	51
Chittagong	22° 21'	91° 50'	+37	20	—1	0
Chittaranjan	23° 50'	86° 50'	+17	20	—0	57
Cochin	9° 57'	76° 15'	—25	0	—0	50
Coimbatore	11° 0'	76° 56'	—22	16	—0	51
Cooch Bihar	26° 19'	89° 28'	+27	52	—0	59
Cuddapah	14° 27'	78° 50'	—14	40	—0	52

1	2	3	4		5	
Cuttack	20° 29'	85° 52'	+13	28	—0	56
Darjeeling	27° 3'	88° 16'	+23	4	—0	58
Dehra Dun	30° 19'	78° 3'	—17	48	—0	51
Delhi	28° 39'	77° 13'	—21	8	—0	51
Dhanbad	23° 48'	86° 27'	+15	48	—0	57
Dharwar	15° 28'	75° 1'	—29	56	—0	49
Dibrugarh	27° 29'	94° 55'	+49	40	—1	2
Durgapur	23° 30'	87° 20'	+19	20	—0	57
Dwarka	22° 14'	68° 58'	—54	8	—0	45
Eluru	16° 43'	81° 9'	—5	24	—0	53
Ernakulam	9° 59'	76° 18'	—24	48	—0	50
Ferozepore	30° 56'	74° 40'	—31	20	—0	49
Gangtok (Sikkim)	27° 21'	88° 36'	+24	24	—0	58
Gauhati	26° 10'	91° 45'	+37	0	—1	0
Gaya	24° 48'	85° 1'	+10	4	—0	56
Gorakhpur	26° 46'	83° 22'	+ 3	28	—0	55
Guntur	16° 19'	80° 26'	— 8	16	—0	53
Gwalior	26° 13'	78° 10'	—17	20	—0	51
Hardwar	29° 56'	78° 8'	—17	28	—0	51
Hazaribagh	23° 59'	85° 22'	+11	28	—0	56
Hooghly	22° 57'	88° 23'	+23	32	—0	58
Hoshiarpur	31° 32'	75° 57'	—26	12	—0	50

Hyderabad	17° 26'	78° 27'	—16	12	0	52
Indore	22° 43'	75° 51'	—26	36	0	50
Jabalpur	23° 9'	79° 57'	—10	12	0	53
Jaipur	26° 55'	75° 49'	—26	44	0	50
Jalpaiguri	26° 32'	88° 44'	+24	56	0	58
Jammu	32° 44'	74° 52'	—30	32	0	49
Jamshedpur	22° 48'	86° 11'	+14	44	0	57
Jhansi	25° 27'	78° 33'	—15	48	0	52
Jodhpur	26° 18'	73° 2'	—37	52	0	48
Jullundur	31° 20'	75° 34'	—27	44	0	50
Junagadh	21° 33'	70° 30'	—48	0	0	46
Kakinada	16° 57'	82° 13'	—1	8	0	54
Kanchipuram	12° 50'	79° 42'	—11	12	0	52
Kanpur	25° 29'	80° 21'	—8	36	0	53
Karikal	10° 56'	79° 51'	—10	36	0	52
Katihar	25° 34'	87° 34'	+20	16	0	58
Kathmandu	27° 42'	85° 12'	+10	48	0	56
Kharagpur	22° 20'	87° 20'	+19	20	0	57
Kodaikanal	10° 14'	77° 48'	—20	8	0	51
Kolar	13° 9'	78° 11'	—17	16	0	51
Kolhapur	16° 43'	74° 14'	—33	4	0	49
Kottayam	9° 36'	76° 32'	—23	52	0	50
Kurnool	15° 50'	78° 3'	—17	48	0	51
Kurukshetra	29° 58'	76° 51'	—22	36	0	50
Lucknow	26° 51'	80° 56'	—6	16	0	53

1	2	3	4		5	
Ludhiana	30° 55'	75° 52'	—26	32	—0	50
Madras	13° 4'	80° 15'	—9	1	—0	53
Madurai	9° 55'	78° 7'	—17	32	—0	51
Mahabalipuram	12° 37'	80° 11'	—9	4	—0	53
Mangalore	12° 52'	74° 50'	—30	40	—0	49
Masulipatam	16° 11'	81° 7'	—5	32	—0	53
Mathura	27° 28'	77° 42'	—19	12	—0	51
Meerut	28° 59'	77° 40'	—19	20	—0	51
Mirzapur	25° 9'	82° 33'	+0	12	—0	54
Moradabad	28° 51'	78° 47'	—14	52	—0	52
Motihari	26° 38'	84° 54'	+9	36	—0	56
Multan	30° 12'	71° 28'	—44	8	—0	47
Murshidabad	24° 12'	88° 18'	+23	12	—0	58
Mysore	12° 18'	76° 39'	—23	24	—0	50
Nagpur	21° 9'	79° 5'	—13	40	—0	52
Nainital	29° 22'	79° 27'	—12	12	—0	52
Nasik	20° 0'	73° 50'	—34	40	—0	48
Nellore	14° 27'	80° 0'	—10	0	—0	52
Ootacamund	11° 25'	76° 43'	—23	8	—0	50
Palghat	10° 46'	76° 40'	—23	20	—0	50
Pathankot	32° 17'	75° 40'	—27	20	—0	50
Patiala	30° 19'	76° 24'	—24	24	—0	50
Patna	25° 36'	85° 8'	+10	32	—0	56

Pondicherry	11° 56'	79° 50'	—10	40	—0	52
Poona	18° 31'	73° 53'	—34	28	—0	49
Porbandar	21° 38'	69° 37'	—51	32	—0	46
Port Blair	11° 40'	92° 46'	+41	4	—1	1
Puri	19° 48'	85° 50'	+13	20	—0	56
Purulia	23° 20'	86° 23'	+15	32	—0	57
Quilon	8° 54'	76° 38'	—23	28	—0	50
Raichur	16° 12'	76° 21'	—20	36	—0	51
Rajahmundry	17° 2'	81° 46'	—2	56	—0	54
Rajkot	22° 18'	70° 48'	—46	48	—0	47
Rameswaram	9° 18'	79° 18'	—12	48	—0	52
Ramnad	9° 22'	78° 51'	—14	36	—0	52
Ranchi	23° 22'	85° 21'	+11	24	—0	56
Raniganj	23° 35'	87° 7'	+18	28	—0	57
Rawalpindi	33° 35'	73° 3'	—37	48	—0	48
Roorkee	29° 52'	77° 53'	—18	28	—0	51
Rourkela	22° 14'	84° 52'	+9	28	—0	56
Saharanpur	29° 58'	77° 32'	—19	52	—0	51
Salem	11° 40'	78° 10'	—17	20	—0	51
Sangli	16° 52'	74° 36'	—31	36	—0	49
Shantiniketan (Bolpur)	23°. 39'	87° 43'	+20	52	—0	58
Satara	17° 42'	74° 0'	+34	0	—0	48
Secunderabad	17° 27'	78° 33'	—15	48	—0	52
Shillong	23° 35'	91° 53'	+37	32	—1	0

1	2	3	4		5	
Sholapur	17° 39'	75° 55'	—26	20	—0	50
Siliguri	26° 44'	88° 26'	+23	44	—0	58
Simla	31° 6'	77° 10'	—21	20	—0	51
Srikakulam	18° 18'	83° 56'	+5	44	—0	55
Srinagar	34° 6'	74° 48'	—30	48	—0	49
Surat	21° 10'	72° 51'	—38	36	—0	48
Tanjore	10° 47'	79° 8'	—13	28	—0	52
Tarakeswar	22° 54'	88° 2'	+22	8	—0	58
Tenali	16° 14'	80° 38'	—7	28	—0	53
Tiruchirappali	10° 50'	78° 42'	—15	12	—0	52
Tirunelveli	8° 44'	77° 41'	—19	16	—0	51
Trivandrum	8° 31'	77° 0'	—22	0	—0	51
Tuticorin	8° 49'	78° 9'	—17	24	—0	51
Udaipur	24° 35'	73° 44'	—35	4	—0	48
Ujjain	23° 11'	75° 46'	—26	56	—0	50
Varanasi	25° 21'	82° 59'	+1	56	—0	55
Vellore	12° 56'	79° 7'	—13	32	—0	52
Vijayanagar	15° 20'	76° 30'	—24	0	—0	50
Vijayawada	16° 32'	80° 36'	—7	36	—0	53
Visakhapatnam	17° 43'	83° 19'	+3	16	—0	55
Vizianagram	18° 7'	83° 26'	+3	44	—0	55
Waltair	17° 47'	83° 12'	+2	48	—0	55
Warangal	17° 58'	79° 40'	—11	20	—0	53
Yeotmal	20° 25'	78° 8'	—17	28	—0	51

TABLE 2

Nakshatra Divisions and Vimshottari Dasa

Nakshatra	Sign	Longitude	Vimshottari Dasa
1	2	3	4
1 Aswini	Aries	0° 0'	Ketu 7 Years
2 Bharani	Aries	13° 20'	Venus 20 Years
3 Krittika	Aries	26° 40'	Sun 6 Years
4 Rohini	Taurus	10° 0'	Moon 10 Years
5 Mrigasirsha	Taurus	23° 20'	Mars 7 Years
6 Ardra	Gemini	6° 40'	Rahu 18 Years
7 Punarvasu	Gemini	20° 10'	Jupiter 16 Years
8 Pushya	Cancer	3° 20'	Saturn 19 Years
9 Ashlesha	Cancer	16° 40'	Mercury 17 Years
10 Magha	Leo	0° 0'	Ketu 7 Years
11 Purva Phalguni	Leo	13° 20'	Venus 20 Years
12 Uttara Phalguni	Leo	26° 40'	Sun 6 Years

1	2	3	4
13 Hasta	Virgo	10° 0'	Moon 10 Years
14 Chitra	Virgo	23° 20'	Mars 7 Years
15 Swathi	Libra	6° 40'	Rahu 18 Years
16 Vishaka	Libra	20° 0'	Jupiter 16 Years
17 Anuradha	Scorpio	3° 20'	Saturn 19 Years
18 Jyeshtha	Scorpio	16° 40'	Mercury 17 Years
19 Moola	Sagittarius	0° 0'	Ketu 7 Years
20 Poorvashada	Sagittarius	13° 20'	Venus 20 Years
21 Uttarashada	Sagittarius	26° 40'	Sun 6 Years
22 Shravana	Capricorn	10° 0'	Moon 10 Years
23 Dhanishtha	Capricorn	23° 20'	Mars 7 Years
24 Shathabisha	Aquarius	6° 40'	Rahu 18 Years
25 Poorva Bhadrapada	Aquarius	20° 0'	Jupiter 16 Years
26 Uttara Bhadrapada	Pisces	3° 20'	Saturn 19 Years
27 Revati	Pisces	16° 40'	Mercury 17 Years

TABLE No. 3
Table of Navamsas

	Aries			Leo			Sagittarius		
Mesha	3-20	13-20	23-20	3-20	13-20	23-20	3-20	13-20	23-20
Vrishabh	6-40	16-40	26-40	6-40	16-40	26-40	6-40	16-40	26-40
Mithuna	10-0	20-0	30-0	10-0	20-0	30-0	10-0	20-0	30-0

	Cancer			Scorpio			Pisces		
Karkata	3-20	13-20	23-20	3-20	13-20	23-20	3-20	13-20	23-20
Simha	6-40	16-40	26-40	6-40	16-40	26-40	6-40	16-40	26-40
Kanya	10-0	20-0	30-0	10-0	20-0	30-0	10-0	20-0	30-0

	Gemini			Virgo			Aquarius		
Tula	3-20	13-20	23-20	3-20	13-20	23-20	3-20	13-20	23-20
Vrischika	6-40	16-40	26-40	6-40	16-40	26-40	6-40	16-40	26-40
Dhanu	10-0	20-0	30-0	10-0	20-0	30-0	10-0	20-0	30-0

	Taurus			Capricorn			Leo		
Makar	3-20	13-20	23-20	3-20	13-20	23-20	3-20	13-20	23-20
Kumbha	6-40	16-40	26-40	6-40	16-40	26-40	6-40	16-40	26-40
Meena	10-0	20-0	30-0	10-0	20-0	30-0	10-0	20-0	30-0

TABLE No. 4
Table of Dasa Balances

Degrees;	Sun			Moon			Mars or Ketu			Rahu			Jupiter			Saturn			Mercury			Venus		
	Y	M	D	Y	M	D	Y	M	D	Y	M	D	Y	M	D	Y	M	D	Y	M	D	Y	M	D
1	0	5	12	0	9	0	0	6	9	1	4	6	1	2	12	1	5	3	1	3	9	1	6	0
2	0	10	24	1	6	0	1	0	18	2	8	12	2	4	24	2	10	6	2	6	18	3	0	0
3	1	4	6	2	3	0	1	6	27	4	0	18	3	7	6	4	3	9	3	9	27	4	6	0
4	1	9	18	3	0	0	2	1	6	5	4	24	4	9	18	5	8	12	5	1	6	6	0	0
5	2	3	0	3	9	0	2	7	15	6	9	0	6	0	0	7	1	15	6	4	15	7	6	0
6	2	8	12	4	6	0	3	1	24	8	1	6	7	2	12	8	6	18	7	7	24	9	0	0
7	3	1	24	5	3	0	3	8	3	9	5	12	8	4	24	9	11	21	8	11	3	10	6	0
8	3	7	6	6	0	0	4	2	12	10	9	18	9	7	6	11	4	24	10	2	12	12	0	0
9	4	0	18	6	9	0	4	8	21	12	1	24	10	9	18	12	9	27	11	5	21	13	6	0
10	4	6	0	7	6	0	5	3	0	13	6	0	12	0	0	14	3	0	12	9	0	15	0	0
11	4	11	12	8	3	0	5	9	9	14	10	6	13	2	12	15	8	3	14	0	9	16	6	0
12	5	4	24	9	0	0	6	3	18	16	2	12	14	4	24	17	1	6	15	3	18	18	0	0
13	5	10	6	9	9	0	6	9	27	17	6	18	15	7	6	18	6	9	16	6	27	19	6	0

Mts	Sun			Moon			Mars or Ketu			Rahu			Jupiter			Saturn			Mercury			Venus		
	Y	M	D	Y	M	D	Y	M	D	Y	M	D	Y	M	D	Y	M	D	Y	M	D	Y	M	D
1	0	0	2.7	0	0	4.5	0	0	3.15	0	0	8.1	0	0	7.2	0	0	8.55	0	0	7.65	0	0	9
2	0	0	5.4	0	0	9	0	0	6.3	0	0	16.2	0	0	14.4	0	0	17.1	0	0	15.3	0	0	18
3	0	0	8.1	0	0	13.5	0	0	9.45	0	0	24.3	0	0	21.6	0	0	25.65	0	0	22.95	0	0	27
4	0	0	10.8	0	0	18	0	0	12.6	0	1	2.4	0	0	28.8	0	1	4.2	0	1	0.6	0	1	6
5	0	0	13.5	0	0	22.5	0	0	15.75	0	1	10.5	0	1	6	0	1	12.75	0	1	8.25	0	1	15
6	0	0	16.2	0	0	27	0	0	18.9	0	1	18.6	0	1	13.2	0	1	21.3	0	1	15.9	0	1	24
7	0	0	18.9	0	1	1.5	0	0	22.05	0	1	26.7	0	1	20.4	0	1	29.85	0	1	23.55	0	2	3
8	0	0	21.6	0	1	6	0	0	25.2	0	2	4.8	0	1	27.6	0	2	8.3	0	2	1.2	0	2	12
9	0	0	24.3	0	1	10.5	0	0	28.35	0	2	12.9	0	2	4.8	0	2	16.95	0	2	8.85	0	2	21
10	0	0	27	0	1	15	0	1	1.5	0	2	21	0	2	12	0	2	25.5	0	2	16.5	0	3	0
20	0	1	24	0	3	0	0	2	3	0	5	12	0	4	24	0	5	21	0	5	3	0	6	0
30	0	2	21	0	4	15	0	3	4.5	0	8	3	0	7	6	0	8	16.5	0	7	19.5	0	9	0
40	0	3	18	0	6	0	0	4	6	0	10	24	0	9	18	0	11	12	0	10	6	1	0	0
50	0	4	15	0	7	15	0	5	7.5	1	1	15	1	0	0	1	2	7.5	1	0	22.5	1	3	0

Table No. 5
Table of Dasas
SUN'S PERIOD

Sub-Periods

	Sun	Moon	Mars	Rahu	Jupiter	Saturn	Mercury	Ketu	Venus	Total
Years	0	0	0	0	0	0	0	0	1	6
Months	3	6	4	10	9	11	10	4	0	0
Days	18	0	6	24	18	12	6	6	0	0

Minor Sub-Periods

1. M.S.P. of Sun

	M	D	H
Sun	0	5	9.6
Moon	0	9	0.0
Mars	0	6	7.2
Rahu	0	16	4.8
Jupiter	0	14	9.6
Saturn	0	17	2.4
Mercury	0	15	7.2
Ketu	0	6	7.2
Venus	0	18	0.0
Total	3	18	0.0

2. M.S.P. of Moon

	M	D	H
Moon	0	15	0
Mars	0	10	12
Rahu	0	27	0
Jupiter	0	24	0
Saturn	0	28	12
Mercury	0	25	12
Ketu	0	10	12
Venus	1	0	0
Sun	0	9	0
Total	6	0	0

3. M.S.P. of Mars

	M	D	H
Mars	0	7	8.4
Rahu	0	18	21.6
Jupiter	0	16	19.2
Saturn	0	19	22.8
Mercury	0	17	20.4
Ketu	0	7	8.4
Venus	0	21	0.0
Sun	0	6	7.2
Moon	0	10	12.0
Total	4	6	0.0

150

	4. M.S.P. of Rahu				5. M.S.P. of Jupiter				6. M.S.P. of Saturn		
	M	D	H		M	D	H		M	D	H
Rahu	1	18	14.4	Jupiter	1	8	9.6	Saturn	1	24	3.6
Jupiter	1	13	4.8	Saturn	1	15	14.4	Mercury	1	18	10.8
Saturn	1	21	7.2	Mercury	1	10	19.2	Ketu	0	19	22.8
Mercury	1	15	21.6	Ketu	0	16	19.2	Venus	1	27	0.0
Ketu,	0	18	21.6	Venus	1	18	0.0	Sun	0	17	0.4
Venus	1	24	0.0	Sun	0	14	9.6	Moon	0	28	12.0
Sun	0	16	4.8	Moon	0	24	0.0	Mars	0	19	22.8
Moon	0	27	0.0	Mars	0	16	19.2	Rahu	1	21	7.2
Mars	0	18	21.6	Rahu	1	13	4.8	Jupiter	1	15	14.6
Total	10	24	0.0	Total	9	18	0.0	Total	11	12	0.0

7. M.S.P. of Mercury

	M	D	H
Mercury	1	13	8.4
Ketu	0	17	20.4
Venus	1	21	0.0
Sun	0	15	7.2
Moon	0	25	12.0
Mars	0	17	20.4
Rahu	1	15	21.6
Jupiter	1	10	19.2
Saturn	1	18	10.8
Total	10	6	0.0

8. M.S.P. of Ketu

	M	D	H
Ketu	0	7	8.4
Venus	0	21	0.0
Sun	2	6	7.2
Moon	0	10	12.0
Mars	0	7	8.4
Rahu	0	18	21.6
Jupiter	0	16	19.6
Saturn	0	19	22.8
Mercury	0	17	20.4
Total	4	6	0.0

9. M.S.P. of Venus

	M	D	H
Venus	2	0	0
Sun	0	18	0
Moon	1	0	0
Mars	0	21	0
Rahu	1	24	0
Jupiter	1	18	0
Saturn	1	27	0
Mercury	1	21	0
Ketu	0	21	0
Total	12	0	0

MOON'S PERIODS

Sub-Periods

	Moon	Mars	Rahu	Jupiter	Saturn	Mercury	Ketu	Venus	Sun	Total
Years	0	0	1	1	1	1	0	1	0	10
Months	10	7	6	4	7	5	7	8	6	0
Days	0	0	0	0	0	0	0	0	0	0

Minor Sub-Periods

1. M.S.P. of Moon	M	D	H	2. M.S.P. of Mars	M	D	H	3. M.S.P. of Rahu	M	D	H
Moon	0	25	0	Mars	0	12	6	Rahu	2	21	0
Mars	0	17	12	Rahu	1	1	12	Jupiter	2	12	0
Rahu	1	15	0	Jupiter	0	28	0	Saturn	2	25	12
Jupiter	1	10	0	Saturn	1	3	6	Mercury	2	16	12
Saturn	1	17	12	Mercury	0	29	18	Ketu	1	1	12
Mercury	1	12	12	Ketu	0	12	6	Venus	3	0	12
Ketu	0	17	12	Venus	1	5	0	Sun	0	27	0
Venus	1	20	0	Sun	0	10	12	Moon	1	15	0
Sun	0	15	0	Moon	0	17	12	Mars	1	1	0
Total	10	0	0	Total	7	0	0	Total	18	0	0

	4 M.S.P. of Jupiter				5. M.S.P. of Saturn			6. M.S.P. of Mercury		
	M	D	H		M	D	H	M	D	H
Jupiter	2	4	0	Saturn	3	0	6	2	12	6
Saturn	2	16	0	Mercury	2	20	18	0	29	18
Mercury	2	8	0	Ketu	1	3	6	2	25	0
Ketu	0	28	0	Venus	3	5	0	0	25	12
Venus	2	20	0	Sun	0	28	12	1	12	12
Sun	0	24	0	Moon	1	17	12	0	29	18
Moon	1	10	0	Mars	1	3	6	2	16	12
Mars	0	28	0	Rahu	2	25	12	2	8	0
Rahu	2	12	0	Jupiter	2	16	0	2	20	18
Total	16	0	0	Total	19	0	0	17	0	0

154

7. M.S.P. of Ketu

	M	D	H
Ketu	0	12	6
Venus	1	5	0
Sun	0	10	12
Moon	0	17	12
Mars	0	12	6
Rahu	1	1	12
Jupiter	0	28	0
Saturn	1	3	6
Mercury	0	29	18
Total	7	0	0

8. M.L.P. of Venus

	M	D	H
Venus	3	10	0
Sun	1	0	0
Moon	1	20	0
Mars	1	5	0
Rahu	3	0	0
Jupiter	2	20	0
Saturn	3	5	0
Mercury	2	25	0
Ketu	1	5	0
Total	20	0	0

9. M.S.P. of Sun

	M	D	H
Sun	0	9	0
Moon	0	15	0
Mars	0	10	12
Rahu	0	27	0
Jupiter	0	24	0
Saturn	0	28	12
Mercury	0	25	12
Ketu	1	10	12
Venus	0	0	0
Total	6	0	0

MARS' PERIODS

Sub-Periods

	Mars	Rahu	Jupiter	Saturn	Mercury	Ketu	Venus	Sun	Moon	Total
Years	0	1	0	1	0	0	1	0	0	7
Months	4	0	11	1	11	4	2	4	7	0
Days	27	18	6	9	27	27	0	6	0	0

Minor Sub-Periods

1.

M.S.P. of Mars	M	D	H
Mars	0	8	13.8
Rahu	0	22	1.2
Jupiter	0	19	14.4
Saturn	0	23	6.6
Mercury	0	20	19.8
Ketu	0	8	13.8
Venus	0	24	12.0
Sun	0	7	8.4
Moon	0	12	6.0
Total	4	27	0.0

2.

M.S.P. of Rahu	M	D	H
Rahu	1	26	13.8
Jupiter	1	20	9.6
Saturn	1	29	20.4
Mercury	1	23	13.2
Ketu	0	22	1.2
Venus	2	3	0.0
Sun	0	18	21.6
Moon	1	1	12.0
Mars	0	22	1.2
Total	12	18	0.0

3.

M.S.P. of Jupiter	M	D	H
Jupiter	1	14	19.2
Saturn	1	23	4.8
Mercury	1	17	14.4
Ketu	0	19	14.4
Venus	1	26	0.0
Sun	0	16	19.2
Moon	0	28	0.0
Mars	1	19	14.4
Rahu	1	20	9.6
Total	11	6	0.0

4. M.S.P. of Saturn

	M	D	H
Saturn	2	3	4.2
Mercury	1	26	12.6
Ketu	0	23	6.6
Venus	2	6	12.0
Sun	0	19	22.8
Moon	1	3	6.0
Mars	0	23	6.6
Rahu	1	29	20.4
Jupiter	1	23	4.8
Total	13	9	0.0

5. M.S.P. of Mercury

	M	D	H
Mercury	1	20	18.8
Ketu	0	20	19.8
Venus	1	29	12.0
Sun	0	17	20.4
Moon	0	29	18.0
Mars	0	20	19.8
Rahu	1	23	13.2
Jupiter	1	17	14.4
Saturn	1	26	12.6
Total	11	27	0.0

6. M.S.P. of Ketu

	M	D	H
Ketu	0	8	13.8
Venus	0	24	12.0
Sun	0	7	8.4
Moon	0	12	6.0
Mars	0	8	13.8
Rahu	1	22	1.2
Jupiter	0	19	14.4
Saturn	0	23	6.6
Mercury	0	20	19.8
Total	4	27	0.0

7. M.S.P. of Venus

	M	D	H
Venus	2	10	0
Sun	0	21	0
Moon	1	5	0
Mars	0	24	12
Rahu	2	3	0
Jupiter	1	26	0
Saturn	2	6	12
Mercury	1	29	12
Ketu	0	24	12
Total	14	0	0

8. M.S.P. of Sun

	M	D	H
Sun	0	6	7.2
Moon	0	10	12.0
Mars	0	7	8.4
Rahu	0	18	21.6
Jupiter	0	16	19.2
Saturn	0	19	22.8
Mercury	0	17	20.4
Ketu	0	7	8.4
Venus	0	21	0.0
Total	4	6	0.0

9. M.S.P. of Moon

	M	D	H
Moon	0	17	12
Mars	0	12	6
Rahu	1	1	12
Jupiter	0	28	0
Saturn	1	3	6
Mercury	0	29	18
Ketu	0	12	6
Venus	1	5	0
Sun	0	10	12
Total	7	0	0

RAHU'S PERIODS

Sub-Periods

	Rahu	Jupiter	Saturn	Mercury	Ketu	Venus	Sun	Moon	Mars	Total
Years	2	2	2	2	1	3	0	1	1	18
Months	8	4	10	6	0	0	10	6	0	0
Days	12	24	6	18	18	0	24	0	18	0

Minor Sub-Periods

1. M.S.P. of Rahu	M	D	H	2. M.S.P. of Jupiter	M	D	H	2. M.S.P. of Saturn	M	D	H
Rahu	4	25	19.2	Jupiter	3	25	4.8	Saturn	5	12	10.8
Jupiter	4	19	14.4	Saturn	4	16	19.2	Mercury	4	25	8.4
Saturn	5	3	21.6	Mercury	4	2	9.6	Ketu	1	29	20.4
Mercury	4	17	16.8	Ketu	1	20	9.6	Venus	5	21	0.0
Ketu	1	26	16.8	Venus	4	24	0.0	Sun	1	21	7.2
Venus	5	12	0.0	Sun	1	13	4.8	Moon	2	25	12.0
Sun	1	18	14.4	Moon	2	12	0.0	Mars	1	29	20.4
Moon	2	21	0.0	Mars	1	20	9.6	Rahu	5	3	21.6
Mars	1	26	16.8	Rahu	4	19	14.4	Jupiter	4	16	19.2
Total	32	12	0.0	Total	28	24	0.0	Total	34	6	0.0

4. M.S.P. of Mercury

	M	D	H
Mercury	4	10	1.2
Ketu	1	23	13.2
Venus	5	3	0.0
Sun	1	15	21.6
Moon	2	16	12.0
Mars	1	23	13.2
Rahu	4	17	16.8
Jupiter	4	2	9.6
Saturn	4	25	8.4
Total	30	18	0.0

5. M.S.P. of Ketu

	M	D	H
Ketu	0	22	1.2
Venus	2	3	0.0
Sun	0	18	21.6
Moon	1	1	12.0
Mars	0	22	1.2
Rahu	1	26	16.8
Jupiter	1	20	9.6
Saturn	1	29	20.4
Mercury	1	23	13.2
Total	12	18	0.0

6. M.S.P. of Venus

	M	D	H
Venus	6	0	0
Sun	1	24	0
Moon	3	0	0
Mars	2	3	0
Rahu	5	12	0
Jupiter	4	24	0
Saturn	5	21	0
Mercury	5	3	0
Ketu	2	3	0
Total	36	0	0

7. M.S.P. of Sun

	M	D	H
Sun	0	16	4.8
Moon	0	27	0.0
Mars	0	18	21.6
Rahu	1	18	14.4
Jupiter	1	13	4.8
Saturn	1	21	7.2
Mercury	1	15	21.6
Ketu	0	18	21.6
Venus	1	24	0.0
Total	10	24	0.0

8. M.S.P. of Moon

	M	D	H
Moon	1	15	0
Mars	1	1	12
Rahu	2	21	0
Jupiter	2	12	0
Saturn	2	25	12
Mercury	2	16	12
Ketu	1	1	12
Venus	3	0	0
Sun	0	27	0
Total	18	0	0

9. M.S.P. of Mars

	M	D	H
Mars	0	22	1.2
Rahu	1	26	16.8
Jupiter	1	20	9.6
Saturn	1	29	20.4
Mercury	1	23	13.2
Ketu	0	22	1.2
Venus	2	3	0.0
Sun	0	18	21.6
Moon	1	1	12.0
Total	12	18	00.0

JUPITER'S PERIODS

Sub-Periods

	Jupiter	Saturn	Mercury	Ketu	Venus	Sun	Moon	Mars	Rahu	Total
Years	2	2	2	0	2	0	1	0	2	16
Months	11	6	3	11	8	9	4	11	4	0
Days	18	12	6	6	0	18	0	6	24	0

Minor Sub-Periods

1. M.S.P. of Jupiter

	M	D	H
Jupiter	3	12	9.6
Saturn	4	1	14.4
Mercury	3	18	19.2
Ketu	1	14	19.2
Venus	4	8	0.0
Sun	1	8	9.6
Moon	2	4	0.0
Mars	1	14	19.2
Rahu	3	25	4.8
Total	25	18	0.0

2. M.S.P. of Saturn

	M	D	H
Saturn	4	24	9.6
Mercury	4	9	4.8
Ketu	1	23	4.8
Venus	5	2	0.0
Sun	1	15	14.4
Moon	2	16	0.0
Mars	1	23	4.8
Rahu	4	16	19.2
Jupiter	4	1	14.4
Total	30	12	0.0

3. M.S.P. of Mercury

	M	D	H
Mercury	3	25	14.4
Ketu	1	17	14.4
Venus	4	16	0.0
Sun	1	10	19.2
Moon	2	8	0.0
Mars	1	17	14.4
Rahu	4	2	9.6
Jupiter	3	18	19.2
Saturn	4	9	4.8
Total	27	6	0.0

4. M.S.P. of Ketu

	M	D	H
Ketu	0	19	14.4
Venus	1	26	0.0
Sun	0	16	19.2
Moon	0	28	0.0
Mars	0	19	14.4
Rahu	1	20	9.6
Jupiter	1	14	19.2
Saturn	1	23	4.8
Mercury	1	17	14.4
Total	11	6	0.0

5. M.S.P. of Venus

	M	D	H
Venus	5	10	0.0
Sun	1	18	0.0
Moon	2	20	0.0
Mars	1	26	0.0
Rahu	4	24	0.0
Jupiter	4	8	0.0
Saturn	5	2	0.0
Mercury	4	16	0.0
Ketu	1	26	0.0
Total	32	0	0.0

6. M.S.P. of Sun

	M	D	H
Sun	0	14	9.6
Moon	0	24	0.0
Mars	0	16	19.2
Rahu	1	13	4.8
Jupiter	1	8	9.6
Saturn	1	15	14.4
Mercury	1	10	19.2
Ketu	0	16	19.2
Venus	1	18	0.0
Total	9	8	0.0

7. M.S.P. of Moon

	M	D	H
Moon	1	10	0.0
Mars	0	28	0.0
Rahu	2	12	0.0
Jupiter	2	4	0.0
Saturn	2	16	0.0
Mercury	2	8	0.0
Ketu	0	28	0.0
Venus	2	20	0.0
Sun	0	24	0.0
Total	16	0	0.0

8. M.S.P. of Mars

	M	D	H
Rahu	0	19	14.4
Rahu	1	20	14.4
Jupiter	1	14	19.2
Saturn	1	23	4.8
Mercury	1	17	14.4
Ketu	1	19	14.4
Venus	1	26	0.0
Sun	0	16	19.2
Moon	0	28	0.0
Total	11	6	0.0

9. M.S.P. of Rahu

	M	D	H
Rahu	4	19	14.4
Jupiter	3	25	4.8
Saturn	4	16	19.2
Mercury	4	2	9.6
Ketu	1	20	9.6
Venus	4	24	0.0
Sun	1	13	4.8
Moon	2	12	0.0
Mars	1	20	9.6
Total	28	24	0.0

SATURN'S PERIODS

Sub-Periods

	Saturn	Mercury	Ketu	Venus	Sun	Moon	Mars	Rahu	Jupiter	Total
Years	3	2	1	3	0	1	1	2	2	19
Months	0	8	1	2	11	7	1	10	6	0
Days	3	9	9	0	12	0	9	6	12	0

Minor Sub-Periods

1. M.S.P. of Saturn				2. M.S.P. of Mercury				3. M.S.P. of Ketu			
	M	D	H		M	D	H		M	D	H
Saturn	5	21	11.4	Mercury	4	17	6.6	Ketu	0	23	6.6
Mercury	5	3	10.2	Ketu	1	26	12.6	Venus	2	6	12.0
Ketu	2	3	4.2	Venus	5	11	12.0	Sun	0	19	22.8
Venus	6	0	12.0	Sun	1	18	10.8	Moon	1	3	6.0
Sun	1	24	3.6	Moon	2	20	18.0	Mars	0	23	6.6
Moon	3	0	6.0	Mars	1	26	12.6	Rahu	1	29	20.4
Mars	2	3	4.2	Rahu	4	25	8.4	Jupiter	1	23	4.8
Rahu	5	12	10.8	Jupiter	4	9	4.8	Saturn	2	3	4.2
Jupiter	4	24	9.6	Saturn	5	3	10.2	Mercury	1	26	12.6
Total	36	3	0.0	Total	32	9	0.0	Total	13	9	0.0

4. M.S.P. of Venus	M	D	H
Venus	6	10	0.0
Sun	1	27	0.0
Moon	3	5	0.0
Mars	2	6	12.0
Rahu	5	21	0.0
Jupiter	5	2	0.0
Saturn	6	0	12.0
Mercury	5	11	12.0
Ketu	2	6	12.0
Total	38	0	0.0

5. M.S.P. of Sun	M	D	H
Sun	0	17	2.4
Moon	0	28	12.0
Mars	0	19	22.8
Rahu	1	21	1.2
Jupiter	1	15	14.4
Saturn	1	24	3.6
Mercury	1	18	10.8
Ketu	0	19	22.8
Venus	1	27	0.0
Total	11	12	0.0

6. M.S.P. of Moon	M	D	H
Moon	1	17	12.0
Mars	1	3	6.0
Rahu	2	25	12.0
Jupiter	2	16	0.0
Saturn	3	0	6.0
Mercury	2	20	18.0
Ketu	1	3	6.0
Venus	3	5	0.0
Sun	0	28	12.0
Total	19	0	0.0

7. M.S.P. of Mars	M	D	H
Mars	0	23	6.6
Rahu	1	29	20.4
Jupiter	1	23	4.8
Saturn	2	3	4.2
Mercury	1	26	12.6
Ketu	0	23	6.6
Venus	2	6	12.0
Sun	0	19	22.8
Moon	1	3	6.0
Total	13	9	0.0

8. M.S.P. of Rahu	M	D	H
Rahu	5	16	21.6
Jupiter	4	16	19.2
Saturn	5	12	10.8
Mercury	4	25	8.4
Ketu	1	29	20.4
Venus	5	21	0.0
Sun	1	21	7.2
Moon	2	25	12.0
Mars	1	29	20.4
Total	34	6	0.0

9. M.S.P. of Jupiter	M	D	H
Jupiter	4	1	14.4
Saturn	4	24	9.6
Mercury	4	9	4.8
Ketu	1	23	4.8
Venus	5	2	0.0
Sun	1	15	14.4
Moon	2	16	0.0
Mars	1	23	4.8
Rahu	4	16	19.2
Total	30	12	0.0

MERCURY'S PERIODS

Sub-Periods

	Mercury	Ketu	Venus	Sun	Moon	Mars	Rahu	Jupiter	Saturn	Total
Years	2	0	2	0	1	0	2	2	2	17
Months	4	11	10	10	5	11	6	3	8	0
Days	27	27	0	6	0	27	18	6	9	0

Minor Sub-Periods

1. M.S.P. of Mercury

	M	D	H
Mercury	4	2	19.8
Ketu	1	20	13.8
Venus	4	24	12.0
Sun	1	13	3.4
Moon	2	12	6.0
Mars	1	20	13.8
Rahu	4	10	1.2
Jupiter	3	25	14.4
Saturn	4	17	6.6
Total	28	27	0.0

2. M.S.P. of Ketu

	M	D	H
Ketu	0	20	19.8
Venus	1	29	12.0
Sun	0	17	20.4
Moon	0	29	18.0
Mars	0	20	19.8
Rahu	1	23	13.2
Jupiter	1	17	14.4
Saturn	1	26	12.6
Mercury	1	20	13.8
Total	11	27	0.0

3. M.S.P. of Venus

	M	D	H
Venus	5	20	0.0
Sun	1	21	0.0
Moon	2	25	0.0
Mars	1	29	12.0
Rahu	5	3	0.0
Jupiter	4	16	0.0
Saturn	5	11	12.0
Mercury	4	24	12.0
Ketu	1	20	12.0
Total	34	0	0.0

4. M.S.P. of Sun	M	D	H		5. M.S.P. of Moon	M	D	H		6. M.S.P. of Mars	M	D	H
Sun	0	15	7.2		Moon	1	12	12		Mars	0	20	19.8
Moon	0	25	12.0		Mars	0	29	18		Rahu	1	23	13.2
Mars	0	17	20.4		Rahu	2	16	12		Jupiter	1	17	14.4
Rahu	1	15	21.6		Jupiter	2	8	0		Saturn	1	26	12.6
Jupiter	1	10	19.2		Saturn	2	20	18		Mercury	1	20	13.8
Saturn	1	18	10.8		Mercury	2	12	6		Ketu	0	20	19.8
Mercury	1	13	8.4		Ketu	0	29	18		Venus	1	29	12.0
Ketu	0	17	20.4		Venus	2	25	0		Sun	0	17	20.4
Venus	1	21	0.0		Sun	0	25	12		Moon	0	29	18.0
Total	10	6	0.0		Total	17	0	0		Total	11	27	0.0

7. M.S.P. of Rahu

	M	D	H
Rahu	4	17	16.8
Jupiter	4	2	9.6
Saturn	4	25	8.4
Mercury	4	10	1.2
Ketu	1	23	13.2
Venus	5	3	0.0
Sun	1	15	21.6
Moon	2	16	12.0
Mars	1	23	13.2
Total	30	18	2.0

8. M.S.P. of Jupiter

	M	D	H
Jupiter	3	18	19.2
Saturn	4	9	4.8
Mercury	3	25	14.4
Ketu	1	17	14.4
Venus	4	16	0.0
Sun	1	10	19.2
Moon	2	8	0.0
Mars	1	17	14.4
Rahu	4	2	9.6
Total	27	6	0.0

9. M.S.P. of Saturn

	M	D	H
Saturn	5	3	10.2
Mercury	4	17	6.6
Ketu	1	26	12.6
Venus	5	11	12.0
Sun	1	18	10.8
Moon	2	20	18.0
Mars	1	26	12.6
Rahu	4	25	8.4
Jupiter	4	9	4.8
Total	32	9	0.0

KETU'S PERIODS

Sub-Periods

	Ketu	Venus	Sun	Moon	Mars	Rahu	Jupiter	Saturn	Mercury	Total
Years	0	1	0	0	0	1	0	1	0	7
Months	4	2	4	7	4	0	11	1	11	0
Days	27	0	6	0	27	18	6	9	27	0

Minor Sub-Periods

1. M.S.P. of Ketu

	M	D	H
Ketu	0	8	13.8
Venus	0	24	12.0
Sun	0	7	8.4
Moon	0	12	6.0
Mars	0	8	13.8
Rahu	0	22	1.2
Jupiter	0	19	14.4
Saturn	0	23	6.6
Mercury	0	20	19.8
Total	4	27	0.0

2. M.S.P. of Venus

	M	D	H
Venus	2	10	0
Sun	0	21	0
Moon	1	5	0
Mars	0	24	12
Rahu	2	3	0
Jupiter	1	26	0
Saturn	2	6	12
Mercury	1	29	12
Ketu	0	24	12
Total	14	0	0

3. M.S.P. of Sun

	M	D	H
Sun	0	6	7.2
Moon	0	10	12.0
Mars	0	7	8.4
Rahu	0	18	21.6
Jupiter	0	16	19.2
Saturn	0	19	22.8
Mercury	0	17	20.4
Ketu	0	7	8.4
Venus	0	21	0.0
Total	4	6	0.0

4. M.S.P. of Moon	M	D	H
Moon	0	17	12.0
Mars	0	12	6.0
Rahu	1	1	12.0
Jupiter	0	28	0.0
Saturn	1	3	6.0
Mercury	0	29	18.0
Ketu	0	12	6.0
Venus	1	5	0.0
Sun	0	10	12.0
Total	7	0	0.0

5. M.S.P. of Mars	M	D	H
Mars	0	8	13.8
Rahu	0	22	1.2
Jupiter	0	19	14.4
Saturn	0	23	6.6
Mercury	0	20	19.8
Ketu	0	8	13.8
Venus	0	24	12.0
Sun	0	7	8.4
Moon	0	12	6.0
Total	4	27	0.0

6. M.S.P. of Rahu	M	D	H
Rahu	1	26	16.8
Jupiter	1	20	9.6
Saturn	1	29	20.4
Mercury	1	23	13.2
Ketu	0	22	1.2
Venus	2	3	0.0
Sun	0	18	21.6
Moon	1	1	12.0
Mars	0	22	1.2
Total	12	18	0.0

7. M.S.P of Jupiter

	M	D	H
Jupiter	1	14	19.2
Saturn	1	23	4.8
Mercury	1	17	14.4
Ketu	0	19	14.4
Venus	1	26	0.0
Sun	0	16	19.2
Moon	0	28	0.0
Mars	0	19	14.4
Rahu	1	20	9.6
Total	11	6	0.0

8. M.S.P. of Saturn

	M	D	H
Saturn	2	3	4.2
Mercury	1	26	12.6
Ketu	0	23	6.6
Venus	2	6	12.0
Sun	0	19	22.8
Moon	1	3	6.0
Mars	0	23	6.5
Rahu	1	29	20.4
Jupiter	1	23	4.8
Total	13	9	0.0

9. M.S.P. of Mercury

	M	D	H
Mercury	1	20	13.8
Ketu	0	20	19.8
Venus	1	29	12.0
Sun	0	17	20.4
Moon	0	29	18.0
Mars	0	20	19.8
Rahu	1	23	13.2
Jupiter	1	17	14.4
Saturn	1	26	12.6
Total	11	27	0.0

VENUS' PERIODS

Sub-Periods

	Venus	Sun	Moon	Mars	Rahu	Jupiter	Saturn	Mercury	Ketu	Total
Years	3	1	1	1	3	2	3	2	1	20
Months	4	0	8	2	0	8	2	10	2	0
Days	0	0	0	0	0	0	0	0	0	0

Minor Sub-Periods

1. M.S.P. of Venus

	M	D	H
Venus	6	20	0
Sun	2	0	0
Moon	3	10	0
Mars	2	10	0
Rahu	6	0	0
Jupiter	5	10	0
Saturn	6	10	0
Mercury	5	20	0
Ketu	2	10	0
Total	40	0	0

2. M.S.P. of Sun

	M	D	H
Sun	0	18	0
Moon	1	0	0
Mars	0	21	0
Rahu	1	24	0
Jupiter	1	18	0
Saturn	1	27	0
Mercury	1	21	0
Ketu	0	21	0
Venus	2	0	0
Total	12	0	0

3. M.S.P. of Moon

	M	D	H
Moon	1	20	0
Mars	1	5	0
Rahu	3	0	0
Jupiter	2	20	0
Saturn	3	5	0
Mercury	2	25	0
Ketu	1	5	0
Venus	3	10	0
Sun	1	0	0
Total	20	0	0

4. M.S.P. of Mars	M	D	H
Mars	0	24	12
Rahu	2	3	0
Jupiter	1	26	0
Saturn	2	6	12
Mercury	1	29	12
Ketu	0	24	12
Venus	2	10	0
Sun	0	21	0
Moon	1	5	0
Total	14	0	0

5. M.S.P. of Rahu	M	D	H
Rahu	5	12	0
Jupiter	4	24	0
Saturn	5	21	0
Mercury	5	3	0
Ketu	2	3	0
Venus	6	0	0
Sun	1	24	0
Moon	3	0	0
Mars	2	3	0
Total	36	0	0

6. M.S.P. of Jupiter	M	D	H
Jupiter	4	8	0
Saturn	5	2	0
Mercury	4	16	0
Ketu	1	26	0
Venus	5	10	0
Sun	1	18	0
Moon	2	20	0
Mars	1	26	0
Rahu	4	24	0
Total	32	0	0

7. M.S.P of Saturn	M	D	H
Saturn	6	0	12
Mercury	5	11	12
Ketu	2	6	12
Venus	6	10	0
Sun	1	27	0
Moon	3	5	0
Mars	2	6	12
Rahu	5	21	0
Jupiter	5	2	0
Total	38	0	0

8. M.S.P of Mercury	M	D	H
Mercury	4	24	12
Ketu	1	29	12
Venus	5	20	0
Sun	1	21	0
Moon	2	25	0
Mars	1	29	12
Rahu	5	3	0
Jupiter	4	16	0
Saturn	5	11	12
Total	34	0	0

9. M.S.P. of Ketu	M	D	H
Ketu	0	21	12
Venus	2	10	0
Sun	0	21	0
Moon	1	5	0
Mars	0	24	12
Rahu	2	3	0
Jupiter	1	26	0
Saturn	2	6	12
Mercury	1	29	12
Total	11	0	0

Awaken the Genius in Your Child

Shakuntala Devi

Your child's achieving attitude begins with you.

Teaching your child is important. Teaching your child to think is more important. Thinking is not information or knowledge or being right. Thinking is the skill which unlocks the potential within.

This book will help you — the caring parent — combine the unique knowledge of your child's personality with the latest research on how children learn at each age — from infancy, pre-school and through school. At every stage, the book is designed to enhance your child's concentration skills, problem-solving abilities, creativity, and motivation — the complex dynamics which will translate your child's potential into a brilliant legal mind, a gifted surgeon or a path-breaking physicist.

'... the book is a must for all parents.'

The Statesman